Praise f

END OF THE HOUR

"Her life shattered by the sudden loss of her beloved mother, Meghan Riordan Jarvis walks us barefoot through her grief, across sacred shards of loss, guilt, and hopelessness. From *End of the Hour* we emerge with the fierce tenderness that love and loss require of us. What a gift."

—GLENNON DOYLE, author of *Untamed*, founder of Together Rising

"Jarvis's *End of the Hour* is the rare feat of a book that is at once wise and humble, hilarious and heartbreaking, entertaining and educational. Jarvis's story, a behind-the-scenes look at what happens when a therapist's personal losses bring her to her knees, demystifies trauma and offers readers a radiant dash of hope . . . A page turner that will help readers find the shore of their own lives and the will to paddle forward."

—CHRISTIE TATE, author of *Group*

"A glorious depiction of what it means to be human in this world. Meghan Riordan Jarvis expertly expands the conversation about trauma, both for the patient and for the clinician. This smart, warm, and relatable book challenged my assumptions about what it means to care for ourselves and others. I know it will do the same for everyone who reads these pages."

—CLAIRE BIDWELL SMITH, author of *Anxiety: The Missing Stage of Grief*

"The truth of being human is that there is no level of practice, knowledge, or training that can serve as armor against the experience of loss. In the same way that grief can settle in your bones and blanket your life with prickling heaviness, Meghan Riordan Jarvis has written a memoir that you will also feel in your bones. *End of the Hour* is honest about the deep, dark waters of grief, but you will be grateful for how its vulnerability, warmth, and expertise offer a sense of hope, a life raft to hold on to tightly."
— MARISA RENEE LEE, author of *Grief Is Love*

"This is a beautifully written memoir and poignant journey from loss to hope."
— STEVE LEDER, author of *For You When I Am Gone*

"A candid memoir about trauma. . . . A frank chronicle of healing . . . will resonate with readers in emotional pain."
— *Kirkus Reviews*

END
OF THE
HOUR

A Memoir

MEGHAN
RIORDAN JARVIS

ZIBBY BOOKS
NEW YORK

End of the Hour: A Memoir

Copyright © 2023 by Meghan Riordan Jarvis

All rights reserved. No part of this book may be used, reproduced, distributed, or transmitted in any form or by any means without the prior written permission of the publisher, except as permitted by U.S. copyright law. Published in the United States by Zibby Books LLC, New York.

Zibby Books, colophon, and associated logos are trademarks and/or registered trademarks of Zibby Media LLC.

The author has tried to re-create events, locales, and conversations based on their own memories and those of others. In some instances, in order to maintain their anonymity, certain names, characteristics, and locations have been changed.

This publication contains the experiences, opinions, and ideas of its author. It is sold with the understanding that the author and publisher are not engaged in rendering health, medical, or any other kind of personal professional services in this book. Readers should consult their own health, medical, or other professional before adopting any ideas in this book regarding trauma and grief.

"This Day We Say Grateful: A Sending Blessing" © Jan Richardson from *The Painted Prayerbook*. Used by permission. Read poem in full at paintedprayerbook.com.

Library of Congress Control Number: 2023934633
Paperback ISBN: 978-1-958506-20-2
Hardcover ISBN: 978-1-958506-21-9
eBook ISBN: 978-1-958506-22-6

Book design by Neuwirth & Associates
Cover design by Kelly Winton
www.zibbymedia.com

Printed in the United States of America
10 9 8 7 6 5 4 3 2 1

For my sisters, Sheila and Caitlin

And for Mike

who, as my mother always said,

is much too good for me

AUTHOR'S NOTE

This memoir is a story of trauma. I relied almost exclusively on my own memories. I have used some names with permission, but most have been changed. Any true aspect of my client work represented here was also included with permission. If you are a client wondering if I wrote about you, I did, but only insofar as I relate the humbling honor to know, love, and support your efforts toward change and healing. The clients described here are created from an amalgam of decades of work and do not depict any one person (seriously, it's not you).

PROLOGUE

The old, enormous door was a throwback to days of grandeur. The age when a woman in a hoop skirt clutched a cold glass of sweet tea and glistened delicately behind a flittering fan. I was not that woman. Instead, I stood with sweat pooling at the waistband of the leggings I hadn't changed in days, staring at the door knocker, waiting for it to open. I had barely enough strength to remain upright, let alone walk through the door.

For the sake of simplicity, I'd described it as "trauma camp" when I told my kids I'd be leaving for three weeks.

My driver, whose name I had been given twice but still could not remember, walked past me and pushed open the door. She wandered farther into the entrance, calling out, "Hello? HELLO? She's here," then gestured to the right before leaving me standing awkwardly in the oversized sitting room. My eyes fell on the three large, well-worn leather couches surrounding a giant hearth. A stone chimney extended the height of the vaulted ceiling. My nose caught familiar undertones of pine ash and smoke, but my mind couldn't catch the memory. Despite my exhaustion and the ample available cushions, I did not think to sit down.

A tall, beautiful woman with Botticelli hair swept through the space. I wondered if her red-and-black flannel lumberjack shirt was some kind of uniform.

"Do you want a CD?"

She pulled a slim square from a full shoebox, smiled warmly, and pressed the gift into my hand. I'd learn later that music played a big part in her life.

"I'm Hope."

I quietly echoed her name, "Hope."

She smiled again. "I'm so glad you're here."

There was that same oddly disconcerting phrase the driver had used after I barely managed the kindergarten task of recognizing my own name on the small whiteboard she held at the arrivals gate. Over the next three weeks, I would come to understand those words as the unofficial mantra of the facility. Passed from one patient to the next, "I'm so glad you're here" was intended as a gift—the belief that this was the place where one might be able to heal.

A tiny woman with a white, anime pixie cut and the voice of a lifelong smoker found me next. She may have said her name was Anne, but I did not use it just in case. Gentle but assertive, Anne ushered me into a small office, where I experienced instant déjà vu at the sight of the plush blue bucket chair; high-shine, white-lacquer chinoiserie desk; faux-marble side table; and brass-colored floor lamp that pitched light to the ceiling in a fan shape that made me dizzy. I took the seat Anne offered, searching desperately for memories my mind refused to release. My eye finally landed on a kicked-up corner of the rug under the desk. The name of a popular home store was visible. Like drawers clicking shut, I recognized the decor as a replica of a catalog cover from a few months back. My breath returned. Reality had felt tenuous for days. Finally, here were some dots I could connect.

"We just redecorated," Anne said, following my gaze. Her silver bracelets jangled as she administered my Breathalyzer.

"I don't really drink," I offered stupidly, as if she could take my word for it.

She asked me about my current medications and thoughts of suicide.

"None," I said, "to either."

Anne sat down behind her computer and smiled as she fingerpicked her way through paperwork I'd apparently forgotten to send in the days prior. I watched as her smile drooped, eyes narrowing in confusion.

"This is unusual..." She cocked her head and gave me a side glance.

The inside of my skull throbbed as I turned toward her dangling sentence.

"We have more than twenty people in our system with files connected to your name. Are they clinicians? Would you like your case notes sent to them?" She drew out the last few syllables with suspicion.

Words abandoned me, and I nursed my confusion in

silence. Anne tapped on the screen and, as if to offer an explanation, squinted and began to read out the list. I did not stop her. Like a library's card catalog, each name referenced someone I had once helped into the same seat where I now sat trying to put words to my symptoms of pain and trauma. In a matter of seconds, I'd transformed from a clinician with an intellectual understanding into a woman of embodied knowing.

I shook my head in a small, quick, but not quite embarrassed no. As a therapist specializing in trauma, I didn't have the imagination to even wonder what my patients would think if they knew I was here.

I sat through two hours of signatures affirming what personal history my traumatized brain was able to provide. Anything on a timeline—symptom progression, past treatment, or the last time I'd slept or eaten—had long since fallen through the sieve of what used to be my exceptional memory.

By the time I was shown to my room, my bags had been thoroughly searched and my things placed in tidy piles on the bed. My razor, tweezers, and cell phone were confiscated as contraband. I was neither annoyed nor shocked. This was protocol. I was, however, surprised to discover that I would have a roommate. The two queen beds, set side by side facing the Jack and Jill bathroom, were a mirror of the suite on the other side of the wall.

I sat down on the bed, eyes moist, unsure what to do next. The room began to fill with the ambient noise of people in motion—distant, then approaching. Warm laughter spilled through the door, and I found a smiling woman who declared with a twang in her voice that she was my roommate. She also reported she was "so glad" I'd come. I wanted her to never stop talking and to please go away, immediately.

"I'm Rachel," she said, extending her hand. I took it and, as soon as I did, began to weep. She gingerly pried my fingers from her palm and looked at me. She seemed concerned, but not overly, and offered me a generous lie that on her first day she had behaved the same way. I lay down on the bed, and she gently pulled the shoes from my feet, explaining that the building was slippers only. There were some for me in the closet. Had I eaten lunch? Did I want a glass of water? Her tone reminded me that we are mothered by many women across the arc of our lives. Later, she would explain and repeat my schedule to me as blocks of time with places to be, classes and sessions, much like college.

For now, she knelt and looked me in the eye.

"Have you met anyone else yet? Do other clients know you've arrived?" she asked.

"Hope?" I offered. Had she even been real? I wondered if I could trust my mind or my mouth to relay my thoughts.

It had been two years since my father's death and two months since my mother's. I had lost more than my bearings— I could barely recall the version of myself who used to spend most of the day attending to the needs of others. The amount of help I now required both stunned and scared me. I had somehow become my first and only problem—my sole responsibility. That I would one day refer to this as one of the proudest of my life was not yet possible to imagine.

Instead, I put my head down on the pillow and slowly closed

my eyes. Inside my head I saw only shapes in gray scale. Pulling the fluffy duvet across my body, the sleep that had eluded me for days finally found me.

My mind offered a last question: How on earth had I let this happen to me?

ONE

By the summer of 1983, I already had a few months practice at being nine. I was finally old enough to join in the big-kid activities during our family's annual summer vacation to Cape Cod. Monday, Wednesday, and Friday I learned to sail in a boat as big as a bathtub, and Tuesday and Thursday I took swim lessons from a teenager who doubled as an occasional evening babysitter.

On an otherwise unremarkable Tuesday, I biked home from the public beach, still wet in my favorite red bathing suit with the side circle cutouts, and found my mother stepping out the door with my little brother and sister. In the family lineup, I was smack-dab in the middle of every kind of sibling a kid could want or resent. I had a younger brother and sister as well as an older sister and two older brothers, one of whom was currently at his job stocking the not-so-nearby grocery store's shelves. Clipping my two-year-old sister into the denim stroller with the rainbow piping I inexplicably envied, my mother offered to let me stay home alone or walk with them from our small bungalow to meet my other siblings at the tiny family beach that was slightly closer to our house. I dropped my bike in the front yard's burnt-orange pine needles, switched out my wet towel for a sun-dried one, and ran to catch up. We all played I Spy as we walked down the long hill to the beach.

I'd just transferred my toddling little sister's hand back to my mother's when, out of nowhere, I felt a foot smack my behind. I swung around in fury expecting to see one of my older siblings, but instead I caught the irresistible toothy smile of my friend Pam's brother as he blurred by on his bike. Chris was sixteen and friends with my older brother and sister. I knew him as my cool, soft-spoken sailing instructor. I grinned back and yelled a flattered "Hi" to the towel around the back of his neck as he squeaked the brakes of his ten-speed down the long, steep hill.

At the beach we did what we always did—swam, reapplied sunscreen, bickered, and built dribble castles until it was time to head back, exhausted, for an early, messy, dinner of fried chicken at the picnic table out back. Accustomed to the routine, my brother and sister and I stumbled into the house, hung out our wet bathing suits, and scattered to our various books and toys. My baby sister followed me around for a minute before I snuck across the street to our neighbor's "come over anytime" yard to play Barbies without little grabbing hands. I knew I would be called to set the table eventually.

From the neighbor's yard, I heard more than I saw over those next many minutes. First, the sounds of my oldest brother rushing into the house and yelling for my mother, then the screen door slapping shut and car doors slamming. The town fire station's air-raid siren blasted the emergency signal as it did every day at noon or anytime the rescue squad was deployed. I listened as our family's car peeled out over the crushed-shell driveway.

Hidden behind the tall hedges of my neighbors' yard, I imagined myself tearing across the asphalt, down the rough stone street, and back into whatever had just befallen my family, but instead, I remained frozen. I felt the inside of my tiny chest cavity detonate into a thousand bees. I did not yet understand I would become both the hive and the keeper of those bees for the rest of my life. It would be years before I grasped the true legacy of the next few minutes—my first "before and after," although I do remember the feeling of safety breaking away from me. From that moment on, I would exist in a different world, where anxiety and fear were my new constants.

It was hours (or minutes?) before our car reluctantly returned, crunching slowly back across the driveway. Two doors opened heavily, but I heard only one close again. Then, like an alarm suddenly waking me from sleep, I heard my name.

"Meghan! *Meg!*" My mother sounded fearfully hoarse.

My legs unlocked, and like Pavlov's dog, I responded to my mother's beckoning. I ran past our car with the passenger-side door still ajar and didn't stop until I found my mother and my siblings in the kitchen—a room much too small to hold us all.

"I need my rosary." There was something wrong with my mother's voice.

She gently moved me to the side while I stood, panting. No one said anything else. My oldest brother sat uncharacteristically curled with his knees bent into his chest and his feet up on the chair. I couldn't see his eyes.

"*What?*" I yelled, surprising myself. My chest thudded, and my ears rushed with the sound of the ocean as the faces of my devastated siblings stared back.

It was my older sister who finally said, "Pam's brother died. He drowned."

She snapped the words at me in what sounded like anger. My mind fell apart. I didn't know a Pam.

"Chris," my middle brother said more softly. "Pat found him when he was swimming after work."

I couldn't take in their words. My Pam? Weren't Pam and I having a sleepover in our backyard tent that night? We'd waited weeks for it to be our turn. I'd been so worried the smell of the hot, crisp nylon would make me too nauseated to sleep. Would she still come over?

Even as a nine-year-old, I knew my thoughts were illogical, certainly too self-centered. The silence that would become my family's main coping mechanism had already begun to seep in. There was no one to explain that the misfiring of my little brain under the pressure of trauma was not my fault. Instead, my guilt over my initial reaction would plague me for decades.

My mother returned from her bedroom, clutching her rosary beads, and pulled us into a circle on the floor. I barely knew the rosary, only the Our Father and the Hail Mary. I felt sick with confusion over the purpose of the prayers. Might Chris still live or were we praying for resurrection? Were prayers similar to magical spells that my lack of attention in church would ulti-mately undermine? With no one to ask, I later drew my own brutal conclusions about who was at fault when all that praying failed to work and Chris remained dead.

Life before Chris's death was a summer spent barefoot on bikes, sharing sunscreen, beach towels, and rides home with neighbors. After his death, the adults immediately traded benign neglect for constant hovering. When I was finally allowed to bike by myself back to Pam's, we sat on swings at a playground near her house, where I stupidly asked how she felt. I remember her slowing the swing, her electric-blue eyes holding mine. "I'm really, really sad," she replied before kicking her legs back to tree height. She didn't ask me how I felt, nor did I expect her to.

I was profoundly confused by how Chris's death seemed significant enough to signal the end of an old life while simultaneously not being worthy enough to mention. Though I was surrounded by people, there was no one I could ask about that paradox. After his funeral, no adult spoke directly to me about his death again until I met my first therapist when I was twenty-three.

My child-sized mind had not been able to manage my overwhelming thoughts and feelings and my parents hadn't known better. General culture insisted it was best to protect children with silence, so I was left to invent my own ways to cope.

TWO

My parents were young when they met. Even when interrogated separately, they kept their origin stories straight. My mother disliked my father the instant she met him. She'd been assigned as his secretary at the St. Louis publishing house where they both worked. It made for an irresistible meet-cute in our family's folklore. He thought she was beautiful and didn't brook fools (true), while she was eventually drawn to his intelligence and ambition. Neither could recall how he managed to win her over. She was only twenty-three to his thirty, but they were both eager for marriage and a big family. Their six Irish Catholic kids were intentional; they both insisted.

Early in their marriage they moved back to the East Coast, where they fell in love again—this time with a farmhouse. My father stayed in publishing, while my mother learned to sew, cook, and manage every manner of repair on a house built in

1799. She made curtains, upholstered chairs, stripped floors, and replaced windowpanes. She brought home guidebooks to identify all the birds, flowers, and plants surrounding their new home. At six feet one inch and nearly a foot taller than my mother, my father handled all the things on high shelves.

Throughout the next decade, my mother invented our family. We were her greatest passion and a complete departure from her own city childhood. We lived in the country, went to school and church, worked hard, played sports, and loved the Beatles. I was sixteen when she finally dropped bread crumbs about her father's temper and her mother's insistence on obedience that could border on cruelty. "My parents probably shouldn't have had children," I heard her say more than once. Her long-held silence generously gave my siblings and me permission to adore our grandparents. When it was her turn, she willed the happy family she'd never had into being. We may not have had much money, but we were lousy with oversized, good-natured chaos and the firm understanding that siblings were meant to love each other.

In the early '80s, my father's ambition and enormous mind landed him a job in New York City, a day's drive from where we lived. I do not know the story of the conversations between my mother and father, only that the five of us stayed behind while my father essentially moved to New York alone, coming home only on weekends. Their decision scripted the rest of our family life and their fifty years of marriage.

As a teen, I was angry and confused by my father's distance. It felt like rejection. One night after a babysitting job, I caught the customary courtesy late-night ride home from the father,

7

who offhandedly mentioned he'd also considered commuting to Manhattan for work. "Your father told me that my children would never forgive me and I'd be an outsider in my own family for the rest of my life." The dad pushed his glasses up on his nose, chuckling at the memory. It was the first time I ever considered that the fault lines running across our family might have caused my father pain too.

Because little was said directly, I translated feelings as facts. Resentment seemed palpable. Mine, my mother's, my father's, though if asked to identify its root, my answer would have missed the nuance that goes into making a marriage and a family. I felt confused about my role in causing or solving the tension but assigned myself responsible. It was a weight that stayed with me for years.

THREE

The transition from our summer cottage back to our three-season farmhouse on the North Shore of Massachusetts was a relief the year Chris died. I climbed into the way back of our car with my green trash bag of clothes and coloring books underfoot. Four weeks after we'd been broken apart by death, my father hugged us goodbye in the driveway before heading south to his New York City job, and my mother drove us north across the Sagamore Bridge. I imagined us returning, catch-and-release style, to another life where swimming teenagers did not die and grown-ups didn't stop talking every time a child walked into the room.

Our farmhouse more than doubled our family's square footage during the non-summer months. Only two hours after we left the summer cottage, we pulled into our driveway in silence and waited while my mother opened the house's heavy blue door to three months' worth of musty, still air. The new, unshakable fear that now traveled with me inspired a security guard–like walk-through inspection of each room. The plush, ancient Oriental carpets laid across the wide pine floorboards felt foreign to my rough summer feet. The space felt stale and empty. Voices were dulled and far away, and every light bulb seemed slightly dimmer. Our house was definitely lonelier than it had been when we'd left it.

The next week, my older sister and brother returned to their boarding schools. In the days leading up to their leaving, I held ice cubes in my hands to dull my new sense of panic at the thought of being separated from them, my older brother in particular.

I insisted on riding with my mother on the hours-long school drop-offs. When asked why, I could not bring myself to admit that my mind seemed to hold only one terrified thought as of late: What if *my* older brother died like Pam's? In the car on the way back, my mother and I sang along to Anne Murray and Barry Manilow; we didn't talk to each other.

Once home, I tried to help my mother any way I could— small tasks like washing a pot, tidying up toys, or getting my little sister off to bed. If my mother noticed, she didn't let on. As the school year began, I'd line up our shoes and backpacks at the front door in the hopes of both mitigating morning chaos and hearing my mom's "Thanks, Meg" that felt like a consoling hand on my shoulder.

Around the same time, also unnoticed by my mother, I discovered the power of sneaking food. Carbohydrates, particularly— bread, chips, and cookies—when eaten rapidly and in bulk, helped to keep unwanted feelings at a distance and seemed to settle my stomach. As the weeks went by, my palliative use of food increased with my waistline.

dress with completely new eyes. I was humiliated by my mistake. The clarity of my friend's unkind words took their place in the pew next to silence and grief.

When the bell rang, I forgot my excitement to learn the name of my new teacher and instead slipped into the side bathroom as the rest of the school filed into the cafeteria.

I used the toilet as a seat and hung my head in my hands, taking the deep breaths I'd already discovered could save me from crying. I understood I would not tell Shelby about Chris, my mom's nighttime crying, or how the summer chart-topper, the Police's "Every Breath You Take," made my mouth taste like metal. I looked down at my new white shoes. A hard black scuff had already darkened the right toe.

By the second week of school, Shelby and I were not friends. We hadn't fought. She'd asked me to play at recess, but I couldn't bear the way it felt to be near her. I couldn't understand how I'd never noticed I was fat before. My shame was instant and insurmountable. With no one to help translate the constant feeling of anxiety that resided in my chest, my weight easily wore the mantle as the reason I felt so different from everyone. I was grateful to Shelby for giving me an explanation where others had been silent. I was chubby all of the time and felt bad most of the time. The emotional math added up perfectly. I was never going to achieve a feeling of competency when I was trying so hard not to feel anything at all.

My homeroom teacher, Ms. Ryan, wrote on my report card that year: "Meghan is a bright but angry child."

We'd been discussing the book *Where the Red Fern Grows*,

which had upset several students with the death of a dog. "It's too sad," my classmate Holly whined.

"You think a dead dog is sad? Kids die, and grown-ups can't keep you safe," I said.

I remember Ms. Ryan's exact reply: "What is *wrong* with you, Meghan? That is enough."

I agreed. It was enough, but during recess I told Holly there was no Santa Claus.

Ms. Ryan was pretty and wore perfume, and I wanted her to like me. I raised my hand with questions I didn't have just so I could walk up to her desk holding my workbook, where I would soak in the scent of her. I could feel her disdain, but couldn't help myself from seeking her approval. Years later, I realized Ms. Ryan may not have hated me so much as feared the exploding vortex of feelings that emanated off me. That my teacher had been impacted by the rule of silence, too, made me feel a different kind of sad.

Outside of school, I spent most of my time at my house, on my own. The siblings who were closest in age were brothers who loved sports, Atari, and various outside war games. I played both sides of Chutes and Ladders and set up activities to keep my little sister out of our mother's hair. I managed to find a perimeter of safety and mostly knew how to stay inside it. Two of my three brothers' bedrooms were in the converted horse barn attached to the house. I became fixated on the four solid wooden doors that closed across the long length of our house between their beds and mine. I'd often imagine a fire breaking out at night and worry that I would not be able to save them. I didn't seem to understand that, being younger and smaller than both of them, I should have expected them to save me.

Grade school continued to be a minefield of misunderstanding that left me isolated and desperate. I started lying, which I later learned is a common strategy among children of trauma. Children create stories to match their elevated feelings, and each of my stories was more amazing than the last—trips to countries I hadn't visited, famous people I'd never met, or physical achievements beyond the capability of any child my age. Kids love a target, and my lies made me an easy one. I quickly managed to alienate most of my classmates. Before long, I was the girl with the note in her desk signed by the entire grade: "We hate you," it read.

A part of me found relief on the receiving end of their cruelty. Like an animal cornered, I stopped fighting or running and just accepted. I understood it was what I deserved. As a middle sibling, I was privy to the ways kids sometimes used exclusion as power, and I had done it too. I despised myself for wanting approval and attention, and I despised my classmates for refusing to concede it. But if they had given me that note, I'd have signed it too.

FOUR

I wasn't sure whether I should tell my father about my mother's nightly crying. It started sometime after we returned from the Cape. I would listen each night, paralyzed, wanting to go into her room and comfort her but knowing she would never forgive me if I did. I felt like we were all hanging on by a thread. Pointing out any fragility, particularly in my mother, might cause the whole system to come crashing down. Pretending everything was okay seemed the safer way to go, but it left me constantly on the verge of panic. Who knew what other dangers were growing in the silence?

Nearly two decades passed before my mother described to me what life was like for her during that time after Chris's death. "I relived it, for so many months, every time I closed my eyes," she told me. I was thirty-six and had just learned about Eye Movement Desensitization and Reprocessing (EMDR), a trauma treatment designed to help the brain desensitize relentless painful memories. My mother stabbed at large chunks of tuna in her salad as she finally shared what I had always known: that every night for a year her memory forced her to watch as the lifeless body of a beloved boy barely older than her own was pulled out from the water. When I told her about the woman who had recently invented a treatment that allowed traumatic images to recede into the background, she gazed off into the distance and said, "I would have liked that for sure." And though I knew better, some part of me couldn't help but take her comment as a criticism.

The weekends my father was home from his job in New York, I sensed more tension in the house. One Saturday morning right before Christmas, my father asked if I wanted to run an errand with *just him*. I was so hungry for his attention that I wasn't even disappointed when we found ourselves at a store that sold specialty light bulbs. My mother would have expected me to stay in the car, but my father beckoned me into the shop. The layers of dust covering the hundreds of chandeliers hanging precariously from the ceiling made my throat itch.

My father passed the broken bulb from the antique lantern that hung over our farmhouse's front door to the shopkeeper. We were assured he had replacements. The old man pointed to a high shelf and said, "Might take a minute." Instead of attending to the task, he leaned across the counter on his elbows and said to me in a stage whisper, "There are *kittens* next door." My nine-year-old eyes bugged with hope as I watched my father tap his fingers impatiently on the counter. We both knew he would be a while, so he nodded to me in silent permission.

I ran to the heavy glass door, pushed through, and skip-stomped to the next store over, where I found mounds of yarn in baskets piled everywhere. There were spools of ribbon organized by size on vertical dowels, creating a small forest of colorful trees scattered across the room. I wound my way through the store admiring the reds, greens, silvers, and golds artfully displayed in long twisted lengths until I came to a settee literally crawling with kittens. I screeched to a cartoon stop, just in time, so as to not disturb the mama cat, who was sleeping in a small basket just at the foot of the couch.

"Did Martin send you?" A woman's airy voice wafted toward me only seconds before her perfume. She moved with effort under her carefully wrapped layers of shawl that could have doubled as a blanket. Wordlessly, she encouraged me to scoop up a kitten. I sat and let my small body sink deep into the well-worn cushions of the couch. As I carefully rubbed the soft clutch of fur climbing slowly into the crook of my neck, the shopkeeper walked back to the counter. The kitten and I sighed deeply, content in the feeling of long-sought-after comfort we'd found in each other.

When my father stepped inside the shop, he shook wet snowflakes from his salt-and-pepper hair. A plastic bag swung triumphantly from his glove. He raised an eyebrow in my direction, and I held out my handful of kitten for him to admire. He put his hand on mine. The outsized motor-like purr shuddered under our palms. I didn't dare ask if I could take it home—we both knew my mother would not appreciate adding a kitten to our story. Instead, my father turned to a basket of yarn on the couch and asked, "Should I get your mom some?" I shook my head. She wasn't knitting at the moment, but he was away too often to know that.

My father wandered to the back of the store, returning a minute later with a delighted "come here" glint in his eye. Still holding the ball of fluff, I followed around an unexpected corner that revealed a perfect child-sized Christmas tree with a beautifully tied fabric bow in a Christmas plaid pinned at the end of every pine branch. Covered in white lights and hundreds of threads of tinsel, the tree glimmered like diamonds in daylight. "What do you think?" my father asked. He was not so subtly offering to trade the kitten for the tree. This was something he *could* get me. My father's tone inflected amusement as he raised his voice to the store owner hidden behind a stack of knitting patterns at the cashier's desk.

"How much for the tree?"

"Oh, that's just a display, dear."

My soaring heart crashed. I had already imagined the tree in a corner of the bedroom I shared with my little sister— my other siblings burning with jealousy. For a second I had allowed myself to think I might share in the shine that seemed to come so easily to everyone else.

I miserably slipped the kitten back onto the couch and followed my father to the register, where the old woman held out a thin spindle with a half dozen spools of ribbons in various shades and widths.

"Which is your favorite, sweetie?" she asked in an overly sweet tone.

"Pink," I said flatly. The old woman pressed the pink spool and a box of straight pins into my hand. She pointed across the street to a hardware store. "They have the mini trees, lights, and lots of tinsel too."

My heart pounded as my father handed over a twenty for the ribbon—a wild sum at that time. I thanked them both and didn't dare ask any questions as we walked back across the slushy street. Our traditional five-dollar Christmas tree was ceremoniously cut down each year after a short trek through a nearby forest, but again my father pulled out his wallet and bought me the perfect tree at my same small height, one box of white lights, and two boxes of tinsel. My stomach lurched at the total, a sum that could have treated all my siblings to a meal out.

"Our secret," my father said as we walked back to the car beaming ridiculously. We would never be able to hide the tree. I smiled into the cold of my passenger-side window and let my breath fog up the glass. To this day the scent of pine evokes a feeling of safety and warmth—the opposite of fear.

Once home, my father and I hid the tree and decorations in my room. He closed the door behind him as I laid out the supplies, turned my clock radio to Christmas music, and spent three hours cutting, pinning, and dripping threads of silver evenly across the small branches. When I finished, my tree was every bit as beautiful as the one in the store, and the tips of my fingers were blistered and tacky with pine sap. I slipped down the back stairs to find my father asleep in the rocking chair he'd made by hand. A creaky floorboard saved me from having to decide if I should wake him.

I couldn't fight the tears as my father and I stood in collective pride of the tree's warm golden shimmer. My mother appeared unexpectedly, padding down the hallway, dropping piles of clean laundry onto unmade beds. All three of us froze. She stopped short when she saw us, and I felt my cheeks flame with shame at the possibility that I'd done something wrong. I saw her meet my father's eye before shaking her head with feigned disapproval. My father shrugged and gave her a warm, boyish grin as she continued down the stairs.

"You didn't even need me, kiddo," he said, his voice thick with admiration. "You're so good at doing things yourself." He bent over and kissed my head. I felt the detonation of the cluster of land mines that lived inside me. I knew I would not tell him about my mother crying herself to sleep or how much I yearned for him to be home. Instead, I grabbed the table scraps of love and comfort he offered and added my signature to the ongoing pledge of silence.

FIVE

By the time I was in eighth grade, I had fully cultivated a confident, responsible, and helpful persona that few bothered to challenge. People were impressed with my caretaking skills, and from the outside, I appeared to be in total control. Underneath the surface I was all anxiety, self-doubt, and self-loathing.

That winter, I was the oldest child still at home and it was decided I would babysit for my siblings while my mother accompanied my father on a weeklong work trip to Spain. They'd traveled together before, but my mother had made it generally clear that she didn't love going. With no regular sitter to turn to, my younger brother, sister, and I had been spread across friends' houses or sometimes sent to the Watsons' farm up the street. This time they wanted me to hold down the fort until my older sister came home from college on the weekend. They believed that at thirteen, I was capable of watching my brother, age ten, and little sister, who'd just turned seven. I was told, not asked.

The sitter job involved waking up my younger siblings for our 6:30 a.m. bus to school, which was located a few towns over. There were no lunches to pack, but there were sports bags to assemble, backpacks to check, and school papers to sign in my perfectly practiced mother's handwriting. In the evenings, we returned to frozen meals, ready to heat on the stove. Once we were fed, I cleaned up and monitored homework, night-time TV, showers, and bedtimes.

Unsurprising to everyone but my parents, things did not go well. After two days, I called my older sister at her college in Connecticut in a panic. I'd expected her to scold me for being overwhelmed, so my eyes pricked with tears when she said she was throwing her books in a bag and would be home a day earlier than planned. She made sure I knew she was missing an exam in the process. I felt terrible and terribly relieved.

When our school bus pulled parallel to our house in the waning afternoon light the following day, my shoulders relaxed at the sight of my sister's car in the driveway. I fell asleep early and easily under the cover of Laura Ashley's pink-and-green rosettes, in my antique twin bed identical to my little sister's across the room.

Sometime after midnight, I woke to yelling. I bolted upright as my eyes caught my little brother's red hair thundering down the stairs. I scrambled out of bed and grabbed my little sister by the arm. I didn't feel heat or smell smoke, but the noise in the house seemed to imply fire.

Or water.

I rushed down the stairs, half carrying my sister, stunned as my feet were soaked with freezing cold water at the bottom. I plunked all thirty pounds of her on a step, where she could stay dry, and ordered her not to move. The sound of gallons of rushing water filled my ears as I tore into the kitchen, where small waterfalls gushed from under the sink and near the baseboard heaters. Standing in the rising water in my bare feet, I should have felt freezing, but I felt nothing.

My younger, but not smaller, brother picked up chairs one-handed and tossed them onto the table and the counter.

"Get anything off the floor!" he barked like a ship's captain. No one in this house got to act their age.

I hadn't even noticed my older sister sitting at my mother's small desk, clutching the phone to her ear.

A plastic Playmobil castle with knights on horses floated past my feet. I picked up a figurine in a slow, stunned movement only to drop it again so I could help my brother drag my mother's expensive area rug, waterlogged with a weight well over fifty pounds, into the sink.

My sister yelled over the din.

"They aren't picking up. I have to go get David." She was referring to our friends' father at the farm up the street.

In a move that likely saved us all, but mostly my parents, my older sister grabbed my little sister, who was still crying on the stairs, and rushed from the house into her frost-covered car. My brother yelled again for me to grab another carpet end, and it was only in yelling back that I finally registered the screeching of the fire alarm that had been ringing at an impossibly loud decibel.

My sister was gone only minutes when red swirling lights announced the fire department's arrival. The long truck idled loudly in the driveway as I let the two rescuers into the house. One man went quickly into the basement and turned a small round lever to the left. The water pressure immediately lessened, diminishing gradually until it stopped. The other fireman pulled a wire out of the alarm box, and the house filled with silence so crisp and cold I could feel it on my tongue.

"You okay?" My first thought was how handsome the fireman was. His voice was deep.

"Yes." I loved him instantly, and I needed him out of my house.

"Where's your mom?" I wondered how he knew to ask for my mom and not my dad.

"She went up the street to get help," I lied without the slightest stutter.

The two men turned their bodies slightly toward the door.

"We've seen a lot of this."

"A lot of what?" my brother asked smoothly. We'd both regained our composure.

"Burst pipes. It's been a really cold winter."

They tipped their helmets, like heroes from a movie, and stepped through the door, back out into the cold, leaving a thirteen- and ten-year-old standing in three inches of icy water.

We all went to school the next day. When my French teacher scolded me for yawning in class, I said nothing—house rules. Even when I uncharacteristically failed the pop quiz in history, no questions were asked of me.

I do not recall a discussion or an apology when my parents

returned. While the calamity of the flood was unique, the expectation that I should handle more than I could was not wholly uncommon. It was hard to know whether my parents' attitude reflected the '80s aloof style of parenting or was a specific dynamic I had unwittingly helped create. In this instance, I shamed myself for my fear and took my parents' lack of concern to mean the problem was with me and not with the adults who had left children holding the bag.

SIX

I was on the front half of fourteen when it was my turn to leave home for boarding school. I was desperate for the promise of change. School was to begin on September 11, 1988. My grandfather died on September 10. The tension in the house that ensued felt confusing; I didn't yet understand that anger could provide cover for sadness, but I did understand that I'd miss the first few days of school. I felt guilty that I was more immediately anxious about school than sad about my grandfather's death.

We somehow managed to run late in our three-car caravan from Massachusetts to my grandfather's wake in New Jersey. The room was overly filled and overly warm when we entered. I leaned over the coffin to kiss my grandfather's dead cheek only because my mother did. His flesh felt like very firm tofu, though I doubt I'd even tasted tofu yet. I knelt in a cloud of powdery rose perfume and call-and-response Hail Marys and

Our Fathers. I recall being handed a laminated picture of my grandfather—the size of a credit card, with a prayer attached. His full name was emblazoned at the top: Daniel Francis Reardon. Papa Frank.

The misspelling of his name was a casualty of his immigrant passage. Like so many, the legacy of his country and kin was stripped away in the arrangement of letters. As a teen I imagined future family trees drawn by descendants confounded by the spelling. My father and his brother and sister had last names that were similar but not the same. Each had made their own attempts to reclaim their heritage—O'Riordan. Riordan.

As would have been expected of an Irish funeral in New Jersey in 1988, the reception was at an Italian restaurant. When they didn't hate each other, immigrants of that era held each other with care and understanding. I slipped into a chair at a table for twelve with a cluster of rarely seen cousins. I liked them immediately. Boisterous and confident, they shared stories of being the grandchildren of proximity—second breakfasts and stolen slices of cheese from my grandparents' fridge on their way to school, a comfortable couch to watch weekend sports, and a refuge from siblings and parents on the hard days. They made affectionate references to our grandfather's extraordinary ears and red hair that had silvered only the week of his death and were dead-on mimics of his gruff demeanor and Irish brogue. There was no price of admission to this comfort club. Our shared name, heritage, and family tree was invitation enough to laugh loud and hard in the face of death, and for the first time, I did.

When I did finally make it to my academic powerhouse of a boarding school, located thirty minutes from the farmhouse, I had not only missed orientation but also a few assignments. My compassionate dorm head, a kind whippet of a man who subbed as my adult support and much-needed math tutor for the next four years, asked two juniors to help me settle in— clothes away, shower caddy sorted. I was grateful for the help.

My first few days at school were not as terrifying as they could have been. Campus visits to see my high-achieving older brothers in previous years meant I was less disoriented than many new students. It had been made clear to me, in the form of loving warnings, that because I was a legacy admission and had less obvious talent, I would have to work harder than my peers. Thankfully, my earliest class of the day was my one strength—English. It was held in a beautiful first-floor class-room with a stunning wooden oval table. The building was so ancient you could smell the heat coming up through the grates in the floor. In the coming years, I'd attend many classes seated around this table, learning the power of discussion, argument, and concession.

My English teacher seemed straight out of central cast-ing. Roundish glasses and wispy dark curls just beginning to gray. A radio voice and rosy cheeks. He wore a tweed vest and dark green wide-wale corduroys without irony. "Everyone here is homesick." His announcement was emphatic. "Your essay assignment: write about home."

I was pretty sure he meant the yellow farmhouse with the blue door, but that wasn't the home I was sick for. I already felt the relief of distance from the panic-filled silence of my childhood and could feel a new kind of internal loosening. Because I couldn't stop myself, I wrote about my grandfather's funeral. It was the closest thing to a family reunion I'd ever known. When our teacher walked the edge of the rounded table, dropping papers in our laps the following week, I looked at my hands. I was afraid that I'd failed and was determined to face my disappointment back at my dorm in private. I watched students flip through pages, assuming they were searching for grades, when suddenly, almost in unison, they shifted focus back to our teacher. "What do you think?" he asked, his gaze landing comfortably not on me.

"I like the dialogue. I could hear the accent." I recognized the smiling girl who sat near me in assembly.

My breath stopped. Had we moved on to the reading? What page were we on? I looked to my left, then right, trying to orient myself, but instead saw copies of my paper.

Each student held the pages titled "Three Hours Home," with my name written in loopy handwriting winking out from the top. My classmates' words swirled around me: "a unique interpretation of the assignment" and "a beautiful example of show versus tell." I choked back vomit. As the middle child in a family of various shining stars—none of them me—I'd broken the pack rules by accidentally exposing myself and becoming identifiable. Out of exhaustion and sadness, I'd slipped and told the truth.

For the brief period it existed, the attention wasn't contained to the classroom. The compliments on my writing extended throughout the English department. Teachers I'd never met introduced themselves. I received an invitation to a small writing seminar with upperclassmen and the chair of the department. Part of me wanted everything being offered, but I startled in the accidental attention like a deer in headlights. I froze as though under attack. When I could move again, I slunk back to the cover of the forest of students and hid among them. I systematically declined every invitation and took care to write basic, uninteresting papers ever after—solid Bs.

During my four high school years I observed the value of expansion. My interests, my curiosity, and my capacity for friendship grew, but I had a hard time fighting the comfort of my typical contraction. I managed to find a small, comfortable amount of attention singing in large choirs, or pretending to be someone else in an ensemble play. I always noticed I was both jealous and curious when my peers, particularly the women, found ways to excel and single themselves out in ways that looked both powerful and pleasurable.

I didn't date, but I did grab the attention of a few emotionally messy boys whose depression felt familiar and drew me in rather than repelled me. My confidence as a woman, along with my writing, remained solidly undeveloped.

In the last week of my senior year, I found myself wandering an otherwise empty art exhibit with my first-semester English teacher. I'd made a good effort to avoid him over the years, but now here we were, paused in front of a provocative tangle of wire coat hangers titled *Modern Times*. We nodded with shy smiles at each other until he broke the silence by saying, "I'd always hoped that you'd continued writing."

Of course, I hadn't. But my tears surprised me.

SEVEN

I chose a small liberal arts university outside of Boston after boarding school. In addition to majoring in English, I elected to join a teaching program of mostly women that promised to graduate me and a handful of others in five years with a master's degree. I liked the security of decisiveness in choosing my path early. I declined most late-night party invitations that marked the college experience for my peers. Instead, I went to bed early, got up early, and taught in lower-grade classrooms around Boston while completing a full complement of course credits. By the time I held my degree in early childhood education in my hands, I was exhausted, unhappy, and done with teaching.

I spent one weekend in D.C. with friends who moved there after graduation, singing karaoke, dancing, and eating late-night pizza on a curb on Eighteenth Street, and set my sights on moving. The contrast between the overly responsible life I'd led in college and the fun that seemed available in the nation's capital saw me spending hours at my university's career center, photocopying a wide variety of D.C. job listings. I faxed my résumé and cover letter to nonprofits and political offices and followed up with friendly phone calls until I finally scored a job as an associate at a "think tank" that focused on social policy and child welfare. With my newly minted master's degree, my task was to read the mail to the organization's MacArthur Genius director who was a bit of a bully and also blind.

My move from Boston to D.C. also took place amid my first real love affair. He was a friend of a friend whom I'd spent only hours with before he relocated to the West Coast. Our relationship developed mostly over the phone and red-eye flights every six weeks. I somehow managed to dismiss his arrogance and dishonesty, and the fact that I'd despised him the first time we met, likely because he was a needed distraction from my loneliness. The romance ended spectacularly when, on a regularly scheduled phone call, he insisted he'd "fallen out of love" with me. He somehow forgot to make any mention of the fact that he'd also recently had a suspicious termination of his employment.

I told no one in my family anything about our breakup except what I couldn't hide. That he was liar and a coward was something I kept to myself for years. Also that I was wrecked by the loss. He was an asshole, but I'd loved him. More important, our relationship had soothed my early-twentysomething anxiety that I would never be picked. I was deeply invested in the promise of a life filled with safety and companionship.

I could feel that my oversized heartache was rapidly

wearing out the empathy wagon with my new friends and coworkers. After catching me crying in the bathroom one too many times, an older colleague whom I adored, and who had been married four times (twice to the same man), slipped me the name of her therapist.

"No shame in it, and she's in network," she assured me. I walked back to my desk and, borrowing from her encouragement, made an appointment for the following day.

My new therapist was beautiful, with an easy smile and an enviable crown of heavily highlighted curls. Callie wore expensive jewelry that suggested she existed in close proximity to money.

I took a seat at the start of our first session, and she asked me, "What brings you here today?" I answered her in one continuous run-on sentence about the demise of my relationship, going on for about fifteen minutes straight until she was forced to interrupt me.

"How do the people in your family handle emotions?"

My answer was simple. "Oh, we are very caring. We always hug and say, 'I love you.' We give each other thoughtful gifts and call on birthdays." I smiled at our picture of familial emotional health.

Callie smiled and dove quick and deep.

"And how do you handle problems; how do you support each other with the hard things?"

For reasons I can't explain, I immediately found myself thinking of the story of the burst pipes. Over the years, the details had been argued across my siblings, told and retold until the story had become wildly funny folklore. And so instead of answering her question directly, I attempted to regale my new therapist with the humorous tale. Callie would not be played.

"Is this a funny story?" Her tone of voice made clear she didn't think so.

I felt my cheeks redden as if I'd been caught in a lie.

"I'm not sure."

"I think you are," she said gently. "When you remember that time, how do you feel in your body?" It took me a second to feel it. I'd spent years cultivating a protective disconnect from my body.

"Terrified. I was absolutely terrified." My fingertips touched my cheek as a newly thawed tear unexpectedly dripped down.

"Of course you were." I met her eyes and saw empathy, not pity.

Callie asked the question no one, including me, had ever thought to before: "Do you know what you were so afraid of?"

My answer was instant, like an emotional calling card I hadn't known I was carrying, with no confusion, no laughter: "Someone dying." My hands were shaking when I said it.

I suddenly felt unable to distinguish the memory of the flood from my present-day breakup catastrophe. They both felt like harbingers of death and destruction.

Week after week and session after session, I fell madly in love with therapy.

After a lifetime of symptoms, at twenty-three, I was formally diagnosed with anxiety and intermittent depression. The diagnostic numbers clearly printed at the top of Callie's invoice made me feel like I'd finally cracked my code. She was the first to explain to me that anxiety comes from the right side of the brain known as the sympathetic nervous system. Childhood trauma, in my case Chris's death, impacted the part of my brain known as the amygdala, causing it to become like an overly sensitive car alarm blasting loud warning signals whenever it was hit by the equivalent of an emotional tree branch. When anxiety gets too high, which in my case resulted in panic attacks, the left side of the brain functions like a trip switch in a nuclear reactor that soothes and cools. Trauma creates hyperalert adults, prone to anxiety and panic attacks. Left unattended, that anxiety frequently tips into depression. It was no wonder I had sometimes suffered from both.

Therapy was both thrilling and terrifying. Callie would sometimes interrupt me midstory to drop a casual stop-me-in-my-tracks sort of question: "Was it always the girls who set the dinner table in your house?" or "What would have happened if you had just stopped helping?" With her genuine curiosity and lack of judgment, she invited me to wonder if the unwritten rules I had followed for most of my life still served me.

A light touch with a quick mind and a good sense of humor, she kept me terrific company as I questioned, challenged, and grieved the many unprocessed emotions from my childhood while helping me navigate the everyday hills and valleys of my twentysomething life.

I was surprised to find that Callie's hard questions also reacquainted me with the joy of my childhood. She taught me that my early unresolved trauma (Chris's death) had me conditioned to experience events through a lens of fear and anxiety. Since I was no longer a child, I now had agency and choice. I had the freedom to remember parts of my childhood that included laughter and a significant amount of play. I was stunned to discover many memories where my mother had been mischief's ringleader. Once I did, it was easy to see her as a woman who felt the spectrum of emotions deeply. She was known for her sense of humor—giggling so hard as she retold a story that listeners had to wait for her to take deep breaths so she could get the words out. We teased her for tearing up over children's books and sappy movies. I could not pinpoint when my ability to acknowledge or participate in my mother's deep capacity for joy had become compromised by my own poor mental health.

When Callie asked, "Do you have a favorite story about your mom?," I had one at the ready. I was about ten and my brother was seven. He was concentrating on homework at the head of our kitchen table, with his back to the island, where my mother was preparing meatballs in an oversized Dutch oven. I passed through the room. My mother caught my eye and made a sort of itsy-bitsy-spider movement with her hands and her always-long nails. I almost missed her incongruous rascal expression.

I watched as she crept noiselessly behind my unsuspecting brother, leaned forward, gently scratched his neck, and whispered "Boo" right in his ear. Books and pencils went flying. My brother was simultaneously out of his seat and on the ground. He was screaming and laughing. We were all screaming and laughing. Tears rolled down her cheeks. The meatballs likely burned.

On April Fools' Day a week later, my brother got her back. He wrapped a simple, tan rubber band twice around the spray nozzle of our kitchen sink that, when my unsuspecting mother turned on the tap, caused an arc of water to hit her directly in the face. It was glorious.

Though I never blamed my parents outright for their mis-attunement to my childhood needs, in therapy I let myself hold them accountable. I could acknowledge that they did the best they knew how to do and allow that it hadn't felt like enough. As an adult, I felt compassion and grief over the amount of fear and anxiety I experienced as a child. It felt like the opposite of the shame I'd carried for a lifetime.

My early years of therapy were particularly hard on my relationship with my mother.

I was still learning to feel and express my feelings. I found myself on calls with her suddenly furious. I would punctuate my anger by hanging up midsentence. Callie introduced me to the concept of codependence, explaining that people who took on adultlike roles in childhood often had a hard time separating their needs and desires from others'. When Callie asked me questions like "What do *you* want, Meghan?" we regularly sat in silence while I struggled to keep myself from first doing the emotional math of what I believed was possible. Often my reply came in a flood of anger and the words "Not this." It took me years to learn to manage my reactivity rather than take it out on others. I am still learning.

About a year into therapy Callie invited me to join a weekly group that included a clutch of women who were slightly older, savvier, and more experienced with therapy than I was. I'd expected a traditional "support group" but found something

I would come to understand as a "process group"—a place to explore feelings with and toward *each other*. Callie's job seemed to be to stir the pot.

"Meghan, I noticed you crossed your arms when Laurie was speaking. Did you have something you wanted to say?"

Called out and confused, my answer was not completely honest. "Nope. I'm good."

"Try starting with, 'When you were talking, I felt...'" Callie prodded. A cold sensation ran down my arms, but I plowed ahead. I did the exact thing I'd been taught never to do as a child—I told people my true feelings.

As a lifelong pleaser, it was scary and infuriating when members of the group were upset with or disappointed by me.

"Only someone who really cares about you and trusts you would bother to tell you they feel hurt by you," Callie once told me as I sat reeling on the sharp end of anger from a fellow group member who was furious because I'd said something that made her feel judged. I had to fight my urge to simply walk out of the room.

"Sometimes we hurt people, Meghan. Sometimes even on purpose," Callie added pointedly. "Because when it comes down to deciding whether you are going to meet their needs or your own, you have to choose yourself."

About two years in, Callie started dropping weighted comments during our sessions.

"You'd make a great therapist." Her tone was even, as if stating fact, but I felt like I'd been called out on a crush. I had already privately begun to wonder what academic route therapists had to travel to allow them to hang out their shingles, but like many children of trauma, I didn't relish walking intentionally toward the unknown. I was loath to go back to school, especially if it meant taking out loans, but as I researched the commitment and cost, I told myself I was just curious and not actually hatching a life plan.

"I wonder how it would feel to know you could be great at something but have fear keep you from even trying," Callie said during one session. I didn't have to wonder. I'd spent a lifetime limiting my desires to the things I was 96 percent sure I could get. If I wasn't confident that I would immediately be good—if not great—at something, I stayed this side of safe and didn't even try. This time, both hopeful and scared, I floated the idea of becoming a therapist by my group. The feedback was resoundingly supportive. The other members graciously reflected ways they felt my passion and skill had helped them grow and heal.

It was largely Callie's insistent belief that I would make a great therapist that motivated me to fill out the application to social work school. I committed to not allowing myself to be consumed by academics. The coursework was tedious but easy. I learned that I could get good enough grades by attending class and completing assignments. I rarely bought textbooks or did the reading. I knew I would need to seek additional professional certifications after grad school, so I balanced classes with an otherwise full life and looked forward to when I would be able to trade my chair as a client for the therapist's.

I was not at all cognizant of the emotional undercurrent that was partially responsible for my desire to become a therapist—a promise of safety and security. In becoming a therapist, I committed to a complicated and imaginary insurance policy that I believed would inoculate me from any additional pain and heartbreak when life inevitably went wrong. As the most highly skilled helper, I allowed myself to feel confident that I would never again be the one who needed help.

EIGHT

I was twenty-six when I met Mike at a concert-nightclub venue. It was the summer between the first and second years of my social work master's program, and I had recently broken up with a sweet man I didn't love. I wasn't particularly interested in getting into a new relationship. Callie insisted that more dating practice would help me discern which men I actually enjoyed being with instead of simply being interested in whether or not they liked me, which I'd learned is a typical drive of children of trauma.

According to Callie, women often married men like their fathers, but my father had never been to a place like the 9:30 Club. The club had become my "come here often" kind of place. I'd made loose plans to meet a friend, but pre–cell phone days meant I didn't have much confidence he'd show. I slid my favorite bartender, Clarence, my gym bag, which he traded for a cold beer in a college-throwback red plastic cup. There were so few people in the audience that I wasn't sure I would bother to stay for the show.

As I looked around, I found a close-talking stranger at my elbow. Everything about the guy was too near and too loud. How well did I know the headliner? What did I think of the newest album? Could I give him a quote for his online magazine?

With the house lights still up and music yet to start, there was no easy retreat. Staring ahead, I saw a tall man in glasses with an easy way about him. He was an understated kind of handsome.

"Sorry, I'm with that guy." I nodded and walked forward with confidence honed from my high school improv class. I stood to the left of Handsome and asked, "Will you talk to me so I don't have to talk to that guy?" I tilted my beer in the direction of the budding journalist. It was my best and only accidental pickup line. Callie took pride that the first thing I ever asked my future husband was for help.

Mike and I had been dating for only a month when I threw out my back minutes into my first big social work exam. I made my painful way back to my Capitol Hill row house rental and called my mother (who implied blame), my sister (who felt helpless and far), and my roommate Sarah (who would come home right away). They were all familiar with my back's penchant for exposing my vulnerabilities at the exact wrong time.

Mike and I had fallen into a recent pattern of phone check-ins over lunch. Lying on the floor with help on the way, I causally called his office looking for sympathy.

"So, you already called your mom and your sister?" he asked when I'd told him the story. He seemed to be focused on odd details.

"Yes?" I replied, vaguely registering a trap.

"Oh," he said flatly.

"What?" I returned with a slight edge.

"Well, I'm just wondering why you wouldn't have called me. I'm here. I could have helped."

When we hung up I was confused and annoyed that Mike didn't seem to know the credo of "Minimize your needs and never ask for help" that I'd been raised on. I mentally added his behavior to the list of reasons I'd tell Callie that Mike and I needed to break up this week.

An hour later, Sarah helped me slowly walk down the block like an old lady with a recent hip replacement. On our return, I noticed a familiar silhouette standing on our doorstep in the distance. My body washed with panic and shame, but by the time I struggled back to the door, I was ready to let Mike in.

In the coming months in social work school, I studied human attachment. I watched a famous video depicting the work of the female researcher (one of the very few) Mary Ainsworth, who observed and coded the behavior of toddlers when their mothers first left the room and then when a stranger entered. Ainsworth's experiment identified three types of attachment: anxious, secure, and avoidant. It immediately clicked that I spent my childhood and adulthood on a pendulum swing between anxious and avoidant—at first I would find myself worried that someone wouldn't like me, but once it was clear they did I felt immediately smothered by their needs and desire for connection and pulled away. Ainsworth and others have a lot to say about the role parenting plays in creating secure attachments, but I knew better than to believe any one emotional variable had created the sum of my motivations and behaviors in relationships, romantic or otherwise.

When Mike asked me to meet him at a friend's dinner party a few weeks later, I tried hard not to be too early or too late. Anxiety keeps a mean clock.

"You must be Mike's girlfriend," Colin said in a heavy English accent, as he greeted me at the front door. I nodded hesitantly. Mike had told me on our first real date that he planned to move back to England before the end of the year. His predetermined unavailability made him feel safer. I hadn't planned on being anyone's girlfriend.

Colin swept me upstairs into a swirl of sounds and smells and an already gathered group that included Mike. Post-its acted as place cards revealing I'd been seated next to our host, which I quickly learned was the best spot in the house. Raucous, funny, and both book and *People* magazine smart, Colin was a charmer.

Mike sat next to a young Japanese woman named Nozomi, who seemed to know even fewer people than I did.

Several chairs down and across the lamb shank from me, I saw Mike and Nozomi engaged in a soft-spoken conversation. "Who's speaking French?" I wondered aloud after my ear caught one phrase, then another. Mike popped up his head the way men sometimes do as a greeting. Colin filled in the gaps.

"Nozomi doesn't speak any English. Her father forbade it.

But she speaks everything else." Colin waved his hand toward her end of the table, where, like a UN delegate's assistant, Mike was simultaneously translating the dinner conversation into French so Nozomi was not excluded. I looked at him with his tie slightly askew under his sturdy wool sweater and my breath stopped in my chest. Mike wasn't translating to seem like the good guy. He *was* the good guy.

In therapy the next day, I told Callie miserably that it was time to put a stop to the whole "Mike thing."

"Why? What went wrong?" Callie asked sincerely. I explained that he was just "too good of a guy." Callie reminded me I also spoke French. Perhaps I would have extended the same kindness if the seats had been swapped? But we both knew I wouldn't have. I would have wanted to be in the conversation too much, greedy for attention and fun, whereas Mike's pleasure came from everyone being comfortably included. Callie raised one eyebrow—a move I've always envied.

"Imagine what he might be capable of with someone he truly cared about?" I looked at my feet as my face reddened. She continued, "I get why you want to break up." It wasn't sarcasm. Callie had been working with me for a long time. She stood to walk me to the door. It was the end of the hour.

"Listen," she said with kindness, "go ahead and break up with him. I can see you are set on it, and with your history, it makes sense." She paused and smiled warmly. "And since it's all doomed anyway, you could always just tell him how you feel— for the sake of the practice."

Back then I trusted Callie's instincts more than my own, so even though I feared my feelings were outsized, and even though I feared he would run before I got to leave, I told Mike everything. His response? "Thank you for telling me." The bastard.

What I didn't yet understand was that Callie's advice would become the road to the secure attachment I'd always craved. Rather than accuse Mike of causing my feelings, I learned to just let him know they existed. Mike learned not to try to fix my hurt and instead to simply care about it. We quickly became nimble fighters—apologies came first, and emotional clarity was paramount.

Mike never did move back to England. Instead, over the next several years we slowly evolved in all the ways a young couple does. Mike was easy to adore. He was brilliant, interesting, and interested. Mike's career brought him to a large international organization that sent him to countries I'd never heard of, led by people whose names I couldn't spell. His ability, steady confidence, and lack of ego earned him the respect of his colleagues and manifested as more opportunity. He had an easy, steady way of caring about me that felt generous and inclusive the way some rich people can be with money.

Still, I found our first year together a veritable fun house of emotions. I would stew in pain I knew he never meant to cause, unable to recover in the way I'd seen others do more simply. My hurts often came with physical sensations—cold rushing down my arms, heat to my face. "Feelings are not facts," Callie would remind me, promising that the sensations were messages written by a scared child who couldn't and shouldn't control the behavior of an adult. I learned to tell Mike how I felt, replacing phrases like "Why are you such an asshole?" with "I need you to know that I feel..."

The answer to many problems, which Callie reminded me over and over, was also the antidote to the poison I'd accidentally kept swallowing since childhood: "Just tell him about your feelings."

Eventually Mike and I moved in together, got married, and bought an apartment. With each major life event, I was both eager and skittish. I was aware I managed with more fear than I saw in my peers, but I felt like the milestones pulled me closer to the bell curve of normal, which was the place I'd always longed to be. When I started seeing private clients in my few hours after my day job as a school social worker, I began additional intensive training in EMDR, sensorimotor psychotherapy, and various mindfulness practices so I could be as informed clinically in the therapies that had helped me personally.

We spent four years growing into our relationship and our careers. Then we decided to try and grow some kids too.

Before our daughter was born, I miscarried ten weeks into a very much wanted pregnancy. I was thirty-three, devastated, and didn't know a single person who'd been through pregnancy loss. Though, of course, I did. Start telling people you miscarried and watch the hands go up.

At the end of a therapy session filled with tears over my irrevocable loss, Callie betrayed me with seven terrible words: "I think you just want your mom." My mom and I were coming out of a stage where we were all knees and elbows with each other—still lots of inadvertent hurts. Mostly, she was just being her direct and opinionated self, and I was being a reactive, defensive asshole, taking half of everything she said as judgment and the other half as ill-informed.

Callie had explained to me that part of breaking old trauma beliefs was challenging them with new behavior. Where I once wouldn't have even *mentioned* my loss to my mother, I now went home, called her, and asked her to come to D.C. to be with me. She, in turn, was grateful and teary. She said she'd wanted to offer but felt she never knew the right move with me anymore. She also said she would be on the first plane the next day. About an hour later, in what will forever have earned him the Nobel Peace Prize of parenting that rests on the mantel of my heart, my dad called.

"Hey, Meg. Your mother told me that you asked her to come down? I just wanted to verify you *actually* want her there before I buy her a ticket." He was six feet one inch tall, 220 pounds, and whispering. I told him I was as shocked as he was, but apparently, my mother was the thing that would help me the most with my grief.

I didn't understand yet that Callie had set me up for what we call in therapy a "corrective experience." My mother hadn't been there for me in past loss, and I hadn't known how to ask her to be. Just making the phone call broke the mold of our old operating system of silence. Callie was banking on my mother and I being able to cocreate something new in our relationship. Therapy had changed me.

I picked up my mom at the airport early the next morning. We hadn't even stopped hugging when she said, "You know your little baby is looking down on you from heaven." I physically cringed. I imploded. Per our history, I didn't say anything at first, and by midday, she had said it five or six times. I knew she meant well. I knew she loved me. I also knew that if I didn't stop her from saying what obviously comforted her but hurt me, the hard-fought place of stability in our relationship would be damaged. I wasn't gentle.

"Oh my God, you *have* to stop saying that!"

"Saying what?" My mother looked shocked and scared by my outburst.

"The heaven thing! I don't believe in it!"

"But you go to church..."

She was as bewildered by my inconsistencies as I was. I crumpled into tears. She quickly told me she wasn't trying to hurt me. I tried to explain that I seemed to have lost my hard-candy coating of protection. I was just *so upset* by everything. My mother said lots of things. The most loving of which was "I'm glad you told me or I would have never known."

I wish I could have come in at a five instead of an eleven. I had spent my childhood trying to protect my mother and my young adulthood resenting her for it, living in fear of what felt like her emotional fragility but was likely actually mine. The trauma therapy I'd done with Callie meant I'd taken years of inventory of every emotion I'd ever tucked away. The purpose of dredging up the past was to process the old feelings with my new skill set, but that wouldn't have been obvious to my mother. She felt the flames of my pain and anger but had no way of knowing the fire would burn away the emotional cage I'd kept myself in and not our whole relationship.

Mike and I were lucky enough to go on to have three kids. Before Lucy, my parents' eighth grandchild, was born, my mother made clear she found the whole going-into-labor drill excruciating. The moment she was alerted that someone she cared about was in active labor, she prayed in terror until the baby and mother were declared safe. My mother had birthed six kids. She was entitled to unhinge a little.

We had more than one conversation where she declared she wished she could be "told after the fact." A week before Lucy was born, I double-checked.

"Okay, lady, so I'm *not* going to tell you when I go into labor, right? I'm going to call you when the baby is here. That's what you want?"

"Yes, please. That will be so much better!"

My contractions began the morning of January 5 (my maternal grandfather's birthday)—ten days early. I labored at home and at the hospital until 4:23 a.m. the next day, when Lucy was finally born by C-section. I waited until 5:00 a.m. when I knew my mother would be awake.

"Good morning." She always answered the phone like she was expecting your call.

"Hey, doll."

"What are you doing up so early?"

"Well, I'm just sitting here holding my daughter." After a few seconds of silence, I heard my mother sob. Deep gasps. "Why didn't you tell me?" She could barely whisper it.

Of course, then I realized that we had gotten it completely wrong. We were ridiculous. I'd somehow again convinced myself I could shield her from worry so she'd get to simply experience the joy. I was only just becoming a parent. I didn't yet understand that worry and fear are the underbelly of love.

Two years after Lucy was born, we had Daniel. Named for grandfathers on both sides, my father referred to him as "Daniel the Great." Two years later, Nicholas, christened Nicky by his siblings, joined the chaos. Though she'd threatened to leave if the baby wasn't a sister, four-year-old Lucy yelled into the phone, "Congratulations, Mommy!" when I called her from my hospital bed announcing the arrival of another brother. My mother told me it was the exact phrase I'd said to her when my younger brother was born.

The years of raising young kids really was as dizzying as everyone promised. Our days were constant feedings of some kind or another, playdates and playgrounds, school days and holidays, bath times and bedtimes. Lather, rinse, repeat. There seemed to be alternately not enough and too many hours in every day.

According to my iPhone, I took 3,551 pictures in 2016, when our kids were four, six, and eight. I was fifteen years into the life led by love and healing that all my work in therapy had promised was possible. Anxiety and depression had truly taken a back seat, and my life felt like its own daily gratitude practice. I counted my blessings—sometimes multiple times a day.

NINE

M ike was out of the country on work travel, the sitter
was home with the kids, and I was sitting on a barstool waiting for a friend while casually reading an
email from my mother.

My dad had been experiencing some pain connected to his
kidney, and my parents had just gotten back some test results.
I noticed my mother's note was longer than usual, the tone flat
with fewer exclamation points.

"Interesting and informative session," the first line read.

As they feared, cancer had been detected. It was small cell,
apparently. They'd met with an oncologist already and chemo
would begin in August. Spirits were good. Though much detail
was included, the stage of the cancer was noticeably omitted.

The next day I hustled out of the house as soon as possible. I had scheduled a professional consultation with an oncologist turned psychiatrist named David, whom I'd met at a

conference two years prior. His office was nearby, but he'd graciously walked over to mine.

Our meeting went by quickly. With his hand on the doorknob, practically out the door, the question came to me: "Hey, you're a cancer doctor," I said casually. "What can you tell me about a seventy-nine-year-old with a recent diagnosis of small cell cancer?"

"Client?"

"Just a guy." I shook my head dismissively.

"At that age, he probably has a year. If they recommend chemo, he shouldn't bother."

"Really?"

David swept his hand through his thick salt-and-pepper hair distractedly. "Well, I would skip it if it were me."

I felt a wildfire of panic ignite in my chest. A cloudy, ice-cold sensation followed, traveling from the top of my head through every cell of my body. I moved slowly, as though underwater. I managed to thank David distractedly as he stepped into the waiting room, where my first patient sat, half hiding behind *Better Homes and Gardens.*

It was three hours before I could take another breath that was just my own. Washing my hands in the bathroom, I stared at my own face while I recalled David's words. I exhaled; the walls began to feel too close. Suddenly needing more air, I tore down the stairs until I found myself on the street, gasping and self-conscious.

I checked my watch; it was three o'clock in the morning where Mike was. Calling seemed unfair. I pulled out my phone. There were no voice mails or texts from any of my siblings.

Maybe I'd misread, misunderstood? I clenched my jaw and checked the email again.

Desperate, I walked into the hipster restaurant responsible for flooding my office daily with the smell of fried food and sat down at the small bar. Despite my three clients yet to come, I asked for a very large gin and tonic.

"A double?" the bartender asked—just like on TV. Fried chicken bubbled in the baskets of golden boiling oil behind him. I nodded. I'm not much of a drinker and didn't know if a double meant twice the size or twice the gin, but I did know my dad was dying.

I called my lifelong best friend, Maia.

Maia is Chris's cousin.

Small towns and shared grief can bond children not just in trauma but in beautiful ways.

"Oh my God, what?" Only Maia could hear chaos in the sound of my breath.

"He's dying."

"Oh, honey." She didn't have to ask who.

I don't remember what was said, only the electric pulse of fear that moved from my stomach up through my chest in rhythmic waves.

I swallowed the gin in two gulps and wiped my grief across a handful of cocktail napkins. Then I pushed myself off the barstool, zipped my emotions back inside, and walked up the stairs to where my client Christina was already in the waiting room.

Christina had originally been referred to me by her primary-care doctor. At twenty-eight, she was physically healthy but had experienced a series of panic attacks so intense they'd landed her in the ER. It took one session to connect the onset of her panic to a sweet and well-meaning boyfriend who had asked her to move in with him. In our second session it became clear Christina's partner wasn't the cause of her panic—her mother was. An only child raised by a single parent, Christina had likely experienced moderate-to-severe anxiety off and on throughout her childhood. The full-fledged panic attacks began after she happily and naively announced her moving plans. Christina was shocked when her mother stopped talking to her and devasted when she read her mother's email accusing her of parental abandonment.

In my private practice, perhaps unsurprisingly, I was drawn to working in the field of trauma—grief specifically. Some of my clients sought me out after suffering single, catastrophic events like earthquakes, tsunamis, or car accidents. But most days I treated people with trauma more like my own, clinically described as "developmental trauma." Many had experienced their own hard things in childhood—abuse, neglect, poverty, being bullied—or more subtle traumas like moving or ongoing illness. My sessions looked less like the stereotypical "talk therapy" I'd had with Callie and included a wide variety of treatments intended to move trapped energies like fear and grief through the body. If someone had opened the door during a session, they might have mistaken it for a modern movement class or physical therapy.

Christina had done well with EMDR in past sessions, so today I pulled out the tappers, small buzzing electrodes you hold in your hands. I asked Christina to concentrate on a painful memory while she received bilateral stimulation to her brain from the tappers. The technique was first used on combat veterans suffering what was previously known as shell shock but later renamed post-traumatic stress disorder (PTSD). The intervention worked well to lessen the sense of fear Christina felt after being screamed at by her mother as a child.

Yesterday, Christina's mother had written to say Christina was not welcome to come home for the upcoming holiday if she planned to bring her boyfriend. The panic that ensued was as bad as any Christina had ever experienced.

Sitting across from me, Christina pulled at the cuffs of her sweater with her fingernails.

"I can't go back to living like that again." Her voice cracked. "I felt like I was dying before."

I nodded.

"Remind me how you manage your panic?" I prompted Christina gently. I'd heard from her psychiatrist earlier that he'd upped her anxiety meds. I encouraged Christina to ground her panic with the tools we'd practiced together.

"I can use box breathing," Christina nearly whispered.

"Yes." I smiled. "What else?"

"My mantra." She nodded as if to approve of herself.

"Which is . . ." I asked, though we both knew the answer by heart.

"I live my life to please me, not to betray my mother. How she feels about my decisions is her problem, not mine." Christina grimaced and continued off-script. "But she makes it seem like my choices are killing her. She makes me feel helpless." Her eyes brimmed with tears.

I leaned forward in silence, waiting until Christina looked up.

"Who is the only person you need to please?" I asked Christina softly.

"Me," she answered immediately.

"And what will happen if you pick *anyone* over yourself?" I kept my words even.

"Panic attacks." Christina barked a laugh and flopped back in her chair. I tapped the end of my nose to indicate she'd found the exact answer.

Christina gave a tight smile. "I don't want this fucked-up relationship with my mother anymore."

I nodded and told her that she made sense to me. Her story, though not mine, felt familiar.

Almost as quickly as it began, we were at the end of the hour.

Christina's tension had visibly lifted. I gave her a warm hug. I knew what it felt like to have to borrow from someone else's hope that things *could* be different, that change *was* possible.

TEN

My father lived one week in December when the poisonous chemo cocktail was titrated perfectly to kill the cancer but not him. The following week he was back in the hospital. The side effects were serious enough that the chemo was out, and the alternate antivirals were in.

I made a call to my older brother to get his take.

"So, this is the end of the line for treatment, right?" I found it confusing that none of my family had said as much.

"It's not great news, but the doctors say the antiviral studies seem encouraging." I couldn't tell if my brother thought I needed a gentler version of the truth.

"Right, but we are only talking about trying to preserve days, not cure."

"Well, nobody knows anything for sure." I felt certain he was trying to protect me, but his words made me feel mildly crazy and more than a little bit alone.

At some point I understood that my mother had assigned herself the role of my father's gatekeeper. Everybody had to go through her to get to him. She seemed reluctant to have visitors. It was difficult to discern whether she was managing her own needs or theirs collectively. I wasn't sure I trusted her to know the difference. When she resisted my requests to visit, I resorted to pretending I was considering buying a summer house around the corner from them on Cape Cod. A realtor friend played along. Who knows? Maybe we all thought I was serious.

When I got to my parents' Cape house, where they'd moved permanently when I was in high school, a man who mostly resembled my father, but with less weight on his frame and hair on his head, greeted me. He seemed concerned about my real estate intentions. Had I researched house prices over the last decade? Cape Cod to D.C. was such a long drive. He wouldn't do it in my position.

I touched his arm when my mother was out of the room and said softly, "Dad, I'm not buying a house." It was a rare moment where his brilliant mind had yet to catch up. "The story just got me through the door."

He drank gulps of air that seemed to make his eyes water. I thought I could see I'd been right in my guess that my father's recent isolation was not good for his mental health. Though it drove my mother a small degree of crazy, my father needed to feel he mattered, which meant he needed more people around him. I understood because this was one of the very few ways in which my father and I were the same.

My mother did her early-bird bedtime routine to his lifetime of night owl. He and I watched some BBC TV together, and then I followed him up the many stairs and down the long hallway to where he'd set himself up in the guest room.

He sighed and held on to the walls as he walked. He needed the water glass and iPad he'd left on the first floor, neither of which he could nor would get for himself. He needed help getting into his pajamas. I tucked him up with the same "Call me if you need anything" I always said to my children at bedtime. Before I made it to the door, he said, "I do need help, Meg."

I wished he hadn't said it. I'd offered, but I didn't want him to need me.

I walked back over to his bed. "Tell me," I said quietly, and he did.

"I can't tell whether your mother doesn't want to understand or can't, but I need more care than she can give."

"I know," I said, and tried to wipe my tears without him seeing.

"I think I need to go somewhere." His voice caught on a sob. I put my hand on his shoulder, and we both took a few breaths. My father finally broke the silence, exhaling the words: "A facility."

"Okay, Daddy." My voice made me sound both like a little girl and like a mother. I could feel the energy in my chest fold like origami into sharp, tight creases. Grief and resignation overlapped. I was grateful my father had spared us both by not using the word "hospice."

In the early days of Mike and me, my father was in town on business and took us to dinner. It was the first time the two men met. My father told all his best and most charming stories. After we'd parted ways, Mike declared him "lovely." I stomped back to our Dupont Circle apartment in silence.

"Aren't you going to ask me what's wrong?" I shouted at last.

"I guess I expected you'd tell me when you were ready." Mike's refusal to be baited by my passive-aggressive antics was both infuriating and a relief.

I was immediately tearful. "You know how hard my father can be for me." I was practically whining. Mike had heard stories of how I often felt minimized by my father's lack of interest in my life, and he had given a perfect example of this at dinner. "I'll never understand why you do your job," my father said. It wasn't a question as much as a declaration of disapproval. Despite knowing my reaction was a sign of old, unprocessed feelings, I heard myself explain to Mike that his generosity with my father felt like a betrayal to me.

"I'm sorry," he said. "I didn't mean to make you feel like I picked your dad over you." He somehow managed to find all the correct words. A few hours later he gave me another gift, though it didn't immediately feel like it.

"I am not saying this to hurt you, but it might." I braced myself for impact. "Dinner was lovely," Mike said again. I bugged out my eyes. Was he serious? He doubled down.

"Your dad was charming, told interesting stories, and paid for our meal. Yes, he asked only one question about me, but you warned me he prefers to talk about himself. I had already accepted it and allowed myself to enjoy that he is an incredibly interesting man." Mike identified the poison and offered the antidote in the same sentence. If I could stop getting caught in old cobwebs of disappointment and accept my dad as he was, I might enjoy myself too.

In the emotional tumbling routine of my father slowly

dying, I did manage to land the dismount from the old pain. I successfully let go of any blame or desire for a different version of a dad. He and I were both grateful when I could just easily and simply sit with him in love.

The morning after my mock house buying, I sat on the steps of the patio with my mother. More holding our coffees than drinking, we danced around my father's health.

"If he thinks I'm spending the rest of my life driving him to appointments, he has another thing coming," she said, blowing across her mug.

I tested the waters. "But what if he can't drive again?"

My mother replied with a look I'd seen a thousand times. It said something between "Oh, please" and "Shut up."

In that one minute, I realized, as I would a thousand times again, that the mind has a vast capacity to resist what it does not want to accept. When denial shows up in my day job as a therapist, I push against it. As a daughter, I sipped my silence.

Over the course of the next hour, my mother woke my father, who didn't know what day it was. She called me upstairs. Quickly and gingerly, I ran through the questions on the mental status exam. My father answered tentatively but was alert enough to conceal he wasn't exactly sure who I was.

He leaned what was left of his weight on me, and we lumbered carefully down the awkwardly steep steps of the old house. My mother was on the phone with the doctor.

"He says—"

I cut her off. "ER, Mom."

My father moaned, in pain or dread, I couldn't tell. They'd been to the ER at least five times in the past month.

In the emergency room with an IV needle in his arm, my father's rapid lab results revealed a toxic potassium level. A doctor nodded me into the hallway, where, for the first time but not the last, I was told I might want to assemble my siblings. I sent a text, conveying the news and promising to update regularly. It took five hours, but my father stabilized and was recommended for a simple surgery to stem a new and painful element of his decline.

For hours I scratched my father's scalp through the hair that had been rapidly growing back since the minute he stopped chemo. I sat at the foot of his hospital bed listening to stories I'd heard a dozen times before. When I gathered my courage and gently asked about his end-of-life wishes, he told me there were some people he'd "like notified personally." At his request, I imported every one of his contacts into my phone, and we went through them one by one, deciding how they should hear of his death. I made notes as he spoke: "Friend from college, lovely guy" or "Work colleague, complete asshole." It took four days, two weekend trips up to the Cape, and in the end I had a list of thirty-three people whom my father wanted to receive the sad news from me. Those days were the most concentrated time we'd ever shared in my life and some of the easiest hours ever passed between us.

For years I had scripted the disconnect, the edge of dislike between my father and me, as his fault. In my middle school years my siblings and I spent hours with him holding court at family meals. He gave lectures on everything from the origin of foods to foreign economies and rarely asked anyone else about their interests. When I was in high school and college, he made clear he despised my politics, more than once berating my leanings as naive and an indication of serious character flaws. For years I felt that the life he seemed to prefer in New York was a rejection of my siblings and me. Though I would have never admitted it, I'd devoted hours of my childhood yearning for the warm, attentive version of my dad. The one who bought the Christmas tree for me in just my size. Though he could be abrasive and tough, he could make you feel as warm as the sun.

With the timing of my father's surgery still up in the air, my mother and I agreed to take shifts staying with him in the hospital. She went home to water her garden while he was rolled to the ER, and I went for a sandwich. I learned later he'd waited alone in a pre-op room for an extra hour while I was eating a melted ham-and-Swiss on a bench next to an overflowing trash can.

I returned early and waited in my father's room until I finally heard the lilt of his charming voice approach. Inadvertently eavesdropping, I heard him sweetly make a dinner order. "Tomato soup would be lovely, thank you." As the nurse wheeled my dad's bed back into place, I found myself startled by a few things: My father was sitting up with color in his previously ashen face. And he was smiling at his nurse, who defied the stereotypical image I had in my head.

The voice from the hallway had given the impression of a person with a slight, unassuming presence. Instead, I found myself across from a hulking six-foot-four man with arms tattooed in multicolored sleeves. Perhaps most surprising were his giant feet clad in peach-colored Crocs with small Disney characters snapped into several of the holes.

"I'm Eliot." He extended a huge hand and a huge smile.

"I'm Meghan."

"Oh, I know, I've heard *all* about you. Someone is enjoying his painkillers." Eliot winked at me and declared he would be back with dinner.

Twenty minutes later my dad was propped up on extra pillows and happily slurping away at his bowl of soup. I texted my mom that all was well and wondered if this evening's golden hour might entice me back to the three-mile run that had been my habit since my teenage years. I'd been mystified by my recent lack of energy or interest in exercise. It would be at least a year before I realized that these weeks and months were like accidentally driving back to a house I'd intentionally left. It wasn't good for me. Silenced emotion and too much time on my own instigated a renaissance of my childhood trauma.

Watching my father eat his soup, which in and of itself felt extraordinary given that his appetite had essentially been destroyed by the cancer, we were both reminded of a happier time.

"Remember that soup we had in that little pub near Blenheim Palace?" I nodded as my memory called up the pictures from my junior year of college in Oxford, when my father extended a business trip to see me. We'd ended up caught out in the rain miles from anywhere until a palace gardener finally took pity on us and dropped us at a local pub.

"God, it was pouring that day," I replied, smiling.

Still half lost in memory, my father grimaced as if he'd eaten something sour. All at once, the room began beeping and flashing and quickly filled with what felt like the hospital's entire staff. I heard screaming, but it took me a full minute to realize the sound was coming from me. I watched my father's frame convulse in a way that felt eerily familiar. My mind was slipping from my body as a memory flashed back to one of my C-sections, when I'd experienced my own wild shaking from anesthesia.

I asked a nurse, who looked more like a camp counselor, if my father was having an adverse reaction to the sedative. She agreed it was possible but wouldn't make eye contact. "We don't know what this is, but it isn't good," she said to the floor tiles. I bit the inside of my cheek so hard I tasted blood.

My father's eyes were laden with so much fear I couldn't take it. I stepped out of the room into the much-quieter hallway and pressed my forehead against the cool wall made of painted cinder blocks. I squeezed my arms in an X across my torso, tapping my shoulders lightly—a trauma technique I sometimes used with clients called the butterfly hug. I breathed deeply. The movements were intended to activate the calming side of my brain, but I couldn't tell if it was working.

In less than a minute, I returned to the beeping, the raised voices, and my father's eyes. I held his hand tight. He spoke through chattering teeth. "I don't want to leave you here alone."

"I called the boys. They are on their way," I lied, referring to my brothers. They were all oblivious, tucked into their homes, hours away.

He closed his eyes.

"It's okay, Daddy. I'll be okay."

He released my hand, and again I walked straight out into the hall and pressed my forehead back to the cinder block. Even with my eyes closed, I felt a presence. I opened them to the quizzical expression of Nurse Eliot.

"You okay?"

"I'm trying to keep myself inside myself," I replied vaguely, hoping to explain what it feels like to disassociate. "I need to be here, now."

"Want me to squeeze you?" His reply was instant. I stared for a few seconds at the yellow-and-blue drawing of a butterfly that took up most of his forearm.

Tears pricked, and I nodded a tiny yes. That was exactly what I wanted, what I needed. I felt hope being pressed back into me with the strength of Eliot's tight embrace. The cloudy vapor that had surrounded my body dissipated, and my energy went from watercolor back to bold permanent marker in a matter of a second.

Hours went by. Every ten minutes or so, I'd see a flash of Eliot's multicolored arms in the sliver of rectangular window in the door. I'd step out into his perfect, breath-crushing hug and step back in, regulated and ready.

It was three o'clock in the morning before the doctor announced, "He's stable."

"He's not going to die?" We were whispering in the doorway.

"No," the doctor answered definitively.

I heaved a deep sigh and slowly stepped back toward my father's bed.

Suddenly the doctor, a young man, someone's son, put his hand on this daughter's arm. For a moment it was as though we were alone.

"He's not dying *today*," he said kindly, "but you understand..."

I nodded because I did.

ELEVEN

When I wasn't flying back and forth between D.C. and Cape Cod, I was still trying to balance my clients and clinical work at home. On one occasion this included taking a tour of a rehab facility in the hopes of finding a suitable placement for a client who was finally ready to start the brave life of living sober.

Treatment centers hold frequent "professionals' weekends" that act as open houses. The facility foots the bill, and interested clinicians visit the property and ask questions about the program. In mid-March I flew across a perfect D.C. spring day to flooding down south. I wanted to know how the space felt—I'd found I had better success supporting clients into treatment if I could describe it from personal experience.

The facility had set up a permanent tent to allow their clients privacy while keeping visitors out of the blazing heat that was typical for that time of year. Yet our group of twenty was huddled toward the tent's center on account of the pounding rain.

There was an open chair next to a psychiatrist scrolling on his phone. He nodded warmly as I smiled and took it.

"I'm Deacon. I can't believe I missed a weekend with my kids for this bullshit." He waved his arm in the general direction of the clinic.

"Not a fan?" I asked genuinely.

He shrugged. "My practice requires I do one of these tours a year. Is it your first visit?"

I nodded.

"Sorry you didn't get better weather. It's usually beautiful." He sighed.

"Those yours?" I asked, pointing to the smiling faces visible on Deacon's phone. He passed it to me so I could better admire his beautiful brood. To reciprocate I handed Deacon my phone and he quickly flipped it back to face me.

"Your dad?" he asked softly, showing me not the picture of my kids I'd intended but one I'd taken in the hospital the week before. My father's eyes were closed in a rare minute of respite from pain, my hand on his head, stroking his hair. The attending doctor had again just said the words "He may not make it," and I'd taken the picture for my siblings just in case.

I cleared my throat. "Small cell" was all I got out.

Deacon pulled off his Elvis Costello–style glasses and rubbed his face. "My mom has dementia. Fucking brutal."

I'd intended to say "It's fine," but the tears in my eyes betrayed me. I nodded instead. I was hundreds of miles away from my father and his illness, but grief does not respect distance or state lines.

Soon an equine specialist named Maggie, dressed in unironic cowboy boots and a hat, motioned the group together. She explained she had planned to show us the facility's outdoor labyrinth, but given the rain, she'd had to move the experience into a nearby barn. As the group fidgeted, Maggie explained what we might generally expect from the activity, and I nursed my disappointment. I'd heard this facility's labyrinth was particularly beautiful. It was rumored to have been paid for by a grateful famous musician.

"A labyrinth walk is an ancient, sacred practice that offers the opportunity to quiet your mind in spiritual questioning or openness." Heads nodded as Maggie continued.

"If you haven't walked a labyrinth before, I'd just ask that you be respectful of other people's experience in the circle. There isn't a right way to do it, but most people find it is very different in a collective than on your own." Maggie motioned for us to follow her.

The group of twenty clinicians shuffled through the mud, past the trailhead marked "labyrinth," to a newly renovated barn where Maggie threw open the doors to reveal a large canvas tarp with a circular, mazelike shape drawn on top. Dim lights and the lingering scent of hay and sandalwood completed the scene.

The tarp reminded me of a child's paint-by-number canvas. I vaguely heard Maggie give instructions to anyone interested in taking more time for their mindful walk to collect at the back of the group. She encouraged bare feet, but given that we'd be walking on mass-produced flooring rather than earth, the ask seemed performative.

I'd had deeply spiritual experiences in beautiful labyrinths out in nature before. I quickly clocked the limitations of this one as subpar. Still, I was a guest, and everyone was doing it, so I fell into the loosely formed line at the front. Maggie placed two small LED candles (not even *real* candles) in my hand and said solemnly, "You will know when to put them down."

I decided I'd hurry through. I'd put my plastic candles in the center and see if there was a cup of hot coffee to be had.

I sighed deeply and stepped my bare right foot onto the mat.

My whole body rang like a church bell struck by lightning. I couldn't breathe or move. Was I the only one who'd felt it? My chest thickened into a block of ice that felt like a blend of fear and dread. Since training in body-centered therapy, I'd become more connected to the messages of joy and pain I held inside, but they often still came as a shock.

The room fell utterly still, completely silent except for the thundering rain on the roof above. I looked down at the small, molded plastic lights in my hand and saw that one was considerably dimmer than the other. Tears inexplicably and immediately leaked down my cheeks as my chest warmed to a liquid sorrow. I pulled the dim light up to eye level and felt a sensation of overwhelming love unfold across my body. I dragged my other foot onto the mat and felt the totality of my grief. Somehow I was holding my father's life in my hands.

My mind interpreted the circle shape of the labyrinth as

a calendar year. In my imagination, the center, the halfway point, was six months.

Nearly shaking with a kind of anticipatory grief, I decided to take my lights to the center of the labyrinth hoping the energy pulsating through my cells might release me. No one was in front of me. No noise or movement behind. I shuffled toward the first switchback and was suddenly frozen again. My eyes fixed on an innocuous spot on the tarp. It was unequivocal and irrevocable; *that* was the place. I stopped breathing and felt the well of pent-up sadness slip out from underneath me.

The hand that held the dim light deadened and began to draw itself toward the floor. I sobbed audibly. I was nowhere near the center, but the pull was too strong. I sobbed again and fell to my knees. Unsure of how long I was kneeling, I was suddenly aware of soft movement behind me. I felt a hand on my head. Tears rained into my hair from above. More hands appeared, and the pairs of feet moving from left to right felt like a spiritual witness.

I practiced resting my hand on the mat while still clutching the candle. Minutes ticked by before I was able to let the light slide onto the ground and rest on its own. The inside of my mind wrote the words so clear I could read them: "Three months." The candle's journey ended at month three on the mat. Wild pain gripped my knees, and I suddenly needed to stand. I rose with an urgency that went against my intense desire to never move. I wanted to stay as close to my dimming light as possible.

Eventually, I forced myself to step back from the candle, repeating the words *I love you* in my head. I closed my eyes, willing myself to turn my back on the light, but I felt terror in leaving it alone. I walked away clutching myself in mourning.

As I made it to the center of the labyrinth, I became more aware of the other participants. Faces deliberately tilted away from me, even as hands continued to reach out. I was offered an ethereal sense of privacy and connection.

For no reason other than I didn't want to carry it any longer, I placed the second light easily in the center of the labyrinth. Both my burdens released, I took a deep breath, hoping for a much simpler return.

A labyrinth doubles back on itself, so I pivoted slowly but with intent. I kept my eyes on my feet and felt a light tingling of fear through my body. As I rounded the curve, I anticipated the cold sear of pain at seeing my father's lonely light again. Instead, I saw the miracle of twelve solid and sturdy flames surrounding one dimming light. The sense of love and connection felt as shocking as my grief.

TWELVE

I'd been napping when my mother phoned. I was flooded with fear as I answered. It wasn't like her to call; her voice was eerily calm. My father wouldn't be transferred home on Friday after all. The doctor couldn't make rounds until Monday morning, but it was all fine. He was fine. She was fine with it. Our family's gene of acquiescing to authority is definitely recessive.

I felt instant rage at the thought of my father living four of the last few days of his life in a rehab hospital staffed by overworked nurses when he could have been home with his family and a view of the ocean.

"That is not what is happening," I nearly yelled at my mother. I hung up and called the facility. The social worker was unfortunately unavailable. Did I want to leave a message? My instinctive fight response is anger. I said I was happy to hold. Or perhaps I could call every three minutes until the social worker was back? Miraculously, she seemed to have just stepped into her office.

I let her explain first. Yes, of course they were very concerned about my father, and everyone wished so dearly he could go home sooner, and the scheduling was unfortunate, but the doctor simply wasn't available. When she paused, I explained carefully I was once a medical social worker. There are rules about the frequency of doctors' visits, and I knew them. "While all of your words seem reasonable, they are completely unacceptable," I told her. "Imagine this is your father dying and the lengths you would go to. I have five siblings all willing to do anything. Please."

In my memory I am formidable, more medical advocate than daughter, but it's possible I was pleading, begging, even.

"I'll call you back in ten minutes," the social worker said.

"I'll call you back in eleven," I replied, and canceled the rest of my day.

The social worker did call back to say the doctor would see him at 8:00 a.m. Saturday morning, and I thanked her. Weeping with rage and grief, I wiped my nose on a tablecloth I would then forget to change for a month. I called my mother, who sobbed in relief and hung up on me. I paused in a moment of gratitude; I'd spent years working with Callie to reintroduce myself to a full spectrum of emotions. Titrated appropriately, anger can be a tool of truth and action.

The morning my father was transferred home, I woke an anxious hour early and waited to hear from my mother. She finally called. Her voice was steady and monotone.

"The doctor is sending us to the hospital. Your dad has a fever. They want to run some tests." My stomach filled with molasses. I felt sure I could feel death. It took minutes of breathing to steady my hand, but I called my oldest brother. He was on his way to my parents' house to help receive the medical equipment delivery needed to help care for my father at home. I diverted him to the hospital. "I think you might be going to help Mom in a different way. You understand?" He understood.

Unable to sit still, my daughter and I drove to a tiny French bakery that wasn't yet open. We parked outside with our windows down. There were no other cars; there was no movement, no noise. Suddenly, I heard a low, familiar kind of hum. I whipped my head around to Lucy.

"Did you hear that?" She nodded.

An unmistakable, dissonant, melodic moaning. I stumbled out of the car in a lunge as the sound got louder. Still not convinced we weren't collectively hallucinating, I asked Lucy again, "You can hear that, right?" She nodded again.

I was already crying, though I hardly realized it. I took out my phone and began to record. In the video, you can hear me say, "How is this possible? It's nine in the morning. We are the only people here." The music gets louder, and the camera settles on a man in khaki pants and a blue shirt, standing at an intersection—playing the bagpipes.

I stood frozen, filming as my daughter slipped her hand in mine. The man played for two minutes and eighteen seconds. When the music stopped, he nodded at us, walked over to a gray sedan, and gently placed his pipes in the back seat. As he drove away, I wondered if it was possible I had summoned him.

Bagpipes are a staple at an Irish funeral.

Incredulous, I sent the video to my extended family that morning. A few hours later I got a text from my father's sister.

"I looked up that song," she wrote. "It's called 'Going Home.'"

A strong dose of IV antibiotics and four hours later, my father finally made it back to his house by the sea.

THIRTEEN

I'd tried to rehearse what it might feel like when my sister finally called and said "It's time." Of course, I hadn't predicted the summer storms that would ground my flight home. Jacked up and singularly focused, I had to rebook my trip to Boston through Providence, Rhode Island, which put an extra day between me and the last hours of my father's life. Our sweet long-term sitter came at 4:15 a.m. with to-go coffee. She handed me caffeine, and I handed off my kids. Mike was still making his way back from a work trip in Paris.

Though I'd run this fire drill smoothly a half dozen times, the morning of my father's death was chaos. I sped in my car, which was nearly out of gas. I watched the flashbulb of a newly installed speed camera pop to life. The airport's park and ride was already full at five a.m. My flight left an inevitable fifty minutes late, which, of course, caused a glitch with my rental car.

"Do you know who you talked to?" The young clerk's thick Boston accent scratched my skin with homesickness. He and I were the only signs of life at Providence's overly lit rental counter. Our two sets of red eyes competed for the title of "most tired." He was sure he didn't have the midsized SUV I'd prepaid for. I imagined an alternate version of myself pounding my fists, tearing the molded seats up from their bolts in the burnt-orange carpet, and hurling them at the large plate-glass window.

"I have no record of your reservation," the young man said for the third time, and I felt the sensation of falling. I suddenly understood I would not make it. My father and I would not get to say goodbye. My body yielded to the truth and sorrow. I shook my head, walked to the row of seats, and sat down heavily. I buried my face in my hands and sobbed until I dry-heaved. When I caught my breath again, I walked with purpose back to the rental counter and asked the kid, who stood absentmindedly checking his phone, to "Give me whatever's left."

Three hours later, after driving through rain in a rental car the size of a dinner roll, I finally sat at my father's bedside holding his hand. He had breath still, but barely.

My father received two visits from priests—a double dose of last rites. My mother said hundreds of prayers while my brother played guitar and I sang James Taylor's version of "The Water Is Wide." It was the same song I'd spent hours singing to my children to lull them off to sleep. Over and over, we told my father we loved him, that we would look out for each other and our mother. If he was conflicted about leaving anything behind, I felt sure it was her.

There was a hospice worker in the house who haunted me like a ghost. More than once, having completely forgotten her existence, I turned to find her at my elbow. A nurse when she started three days previous, she'd been promoted to adjunct family in the intimacy of our untenable loss. When I couldn't take my father's moaning, though my sisters had already borne it for a full day, I asked her, "How do you know he's not in pain?"

"He isn't. I could stab him in the arm with a fork and he wouldn't flinch." Though she seemed impossibly young, her voice was steady. "Do you need me to do it?" She held my gaze and, wearing a sweater inexplicably the exact color of the couch, sat back down and melted into the background.

Our vigil had shifted into an odd space of timelessness when my oldest brother called from his house on the other side of Boston. My mother handed me the phone. I heard my brother's broken voice asking if he should try and drive down as I hurried to the only place on my parents' property with a secure cell phone signal during a rainstorm: the garbage shed. Housing wheelbarrows, garden items, and salt for snow days, the bulk of the space was filled by three large and perpetually smelly trash cans. I stepped inside and out of the rain, assuring my brother he was unlikely to make it in time.

For a few minutes we fell into a surreal conversation about my father's eulogy, which my brother had been trying to write. I heard my older sister calling my name just before her number flashed on the screen of my phone.

"I'm getting a call from the house," I told my brother.

"Pick it up." His tone was urgent. We knew. But I missed it.

"Wait, Meg. She's calling me now." In that quick, confusing way that sometimes happens, he also missed the call.

I stood, wishing I could go back in time rather than back into the house. "Keep me on the phone," my brother said. His voice was breathy.

I smiled weakly to myself, imagining we were holding each other's hands for courage. I walked out of the shed and back up the stairs, watching my phone to be sure I didn't drop the call. My sister was waiting at the door.

"He's gone," she said softly.

"Okay. Okay," my brother said, sounding choked up. No one actually had to tell him, in the end.

"Okay." It was as if this was some sort of chess game and we were required to concede the resignation of our king. My father had almost died in front of me a half dozen times. I'd spent the day racing to be by his side. When he finally died, I was in the garbage shed. He'd slipped out after I slipped out. And that was our forever story.

I found myself wrapped in my little brother's hug when I stepped back inside the house. I realized I was soaked from the storm.

The only promise I'd ever made my father was the thirty-three phone calls to alert his people of his death, and I intended to make them. But first, I went looking for my mother. I found her standing just to the side of my father's body, lightly scratching her lips with her long fingernails as she always did when concentrating. I knew better than to try and hug her.

She looked up at me and shook her head in startled disbelief.

"I'm really going to miss holding his hand," she said with a gulp. Time collapsed, and I was fourteen again, standing on the sideline of my brother's high school lacrosse game. I watched my father reach for my mother's hand, which she pulled away meaningfully. It was a marital smoke signal I feared and judged.

Snapped back to the present, I realized I'd seen my mother countless times sitting with an arm extended across my father's hospital bed, her hand resting in his. I wondered if illness sometimes offers a bridge from there to here.

Almost without thinking, I asked her, "Do you want me to take a picture of your hands together?"

Her head snapped up reflexively with a kind of hard look I couldn't quite place—was it anger or disgust? Her expression settled, and I understood—she wore the face of a woman fiercely *alone*.

My mother dipped her head in an almost imperceptible nod and stepped to the hospital bed, which, like his body, would be removed within the hour. I framed their hands with my phone—bony fingers splotched with age. They fit together with ease, holding fifty years of marriage between them.

For the next three hours, I punched the plastic cube buttons of the old-school landline. Each time someone answered, I nervously twirled the long, curly phone cord and said, "This is John Riordan's daughter. I am not sure if you were aware that my father had been ill, but he died this morning, and he asked that I call and notify you personally."

I was struck by how many of his chosen thirty-three had not been told he was sick or did not understand he'd been dying.

Call after call, just hours after his death, I consoled his colleagues and friends. Only one whom I knew personally asked, "How many calls have you made like this?" When I replied, her voice cracked, and she responded with, "Oh, Meghan, that can't be good for you." Her maternal kindness made my eyes sting, but I kept calling.

All too soon we greeted the gentleman from the funeral home. His attire was an homage to church on Sundays and men for whom a suit is an always but a tie is a maybe. I felt achingly grateful for his tie.

At some point, I crept back into the shed to call Mike, who was still on a plane, or maybe in a cab. I left him a message.

"He died. He's dead. I'm going to stay here."

My cruel delivery gave me unfair relief: a place to offset my pain.

Months later, as I told a new therapist my comfortable version of the story of my father's death, I teared up in earnest. "Mike wasn't there," I told her. I was startled by the swell of emotion in my throat. It was becoming an effort to finish the last turn of my organ-grinder act. I'd perfected my role of the hurt spouse, a thin veil over the truth's sharp edges.

I searched her eyes for affirmation, knowing what she would say because everyone did: "He should have been there." I was the obviously wronged party—the beleaguered griever. My new therapist's eyes were soft, and her voice was warm.

"I see," she said. "So that is the story you are telling yourself. If your husband had been there, you would have felt less pain."

I had been clinging to the belief that my loss could be anything other than *mine*. Mine alone. Instead, she'd handed me all the truth that ever was.

I startled her with my laugh.

"Well, shit," I said, wiping away new tears.

FOURTEEN

Three days after my father's death, I returned to D.C. and an unexpectedly empty house. In a rare miscue, Mike assumed I would want some space before facing the kids, and so he took them to the community pool. I walked the rooms of our small home feeling anxious and alone. The old drumbeat of "I'm not important, and people don't care" began to pulse. In the silence, the impending task of telling my children that their Papa died found me pacing when my husband and kids walked through the door several hours later.

I ushered the little ones, hair still wet from showers, onto the couch, avoiding eye contact with Mike. I did not let him hug me, though I remember he tried. My frenzied need to unburden myself of the death was so great, I worried any comfort toward me would crack me open. It did not occur to me to consult the many psychology texts I had nearly memorized or seek an expert's script on how to tell children about a death. I did not once think to ask Mike to do it. Instead, I just hoped the words tumbling out of my mouth would be good enough.

"You know how Papa has been really sick?"

"He has cancer," Daniel offered. He'd had a six-year-old friend who died of cancer the same summer my father was diagnosed.

"Yes. Well, the cancer made Papa's body sicker and sicker, and when I was home with him just now, something awful happened, and he died."

I remember my words exactly. They were painful for everyone.

Lucy let out an instant wail and flung herself into Mike's arms. Nicholas, too, though his cries seemed more fearful and confused. They both asked painfully obtuse kid questions like "Can we still go to the beach without him?" and crushing others like "Are you really sad, Mommy?" Mike and I took turns hugging and crying with them.

Only Daniel sat in the middle of the couch completely still. I felt drawn to him like a magnet. Eventually he asked, his words drawn out slowly, "Is it okay if I just go to bed?" He didn't wait for an answer and began to climb the stairs to his attic bedroom. At seven, he was so little and so big. I flashed Mike a look, and he shrugged.

I helped gather Lucy into her bed. With a red nose and eyes, she was completely exhausted. I went in and kissed Nicky, who had already been tucked in by Mike, and then climbed the stairs to where Daniel sat on the edge of his full-size, big-kid bed.

"Buddy?" He looked up at me, eyes squinting. "You going to sleep?" He pulled on the knees of his Big Ben pajamas.

"I don't think I'm tired."

"Are you having feelings about Papa?"

"No, I don't really feel anything about that."

I could feel his disassociation like cold smoke filling my own chest. I'd also learned to float outside of intense emotions at about his age. I thought of the many times I'd sat in the car with my siblings as my mother grocery-shopped. I would be suddenly gripped by a thought that something terrible had happened to her. Frozen with panic, I would fix my eyes on the store's electric front door as it swooped open and shut, open and shut, convinced she was never coming out. Like a white knight on a steed, after bearing the terror for just a minute, my head would fill with cool clouds so dense they occasionally made me fall asleep.

In social work school, I learned that disassociation was one of the body's strongest defenses against intolerable emotions— an automatic eject button of sorts. I saw it countless times in my office. One client in particular had eyes that would glaze over as he zoned out anytime my questions tapped a little too close to the death of his older brother. After a few moments he would shake himself back from disorientation and ask, "What were we talking about?"

I knelt in front of Daniel and took his hands in mine. Using a therapy technique called "grounding," I tried to pull his energy back into his body. I put my hands over his and applied medium pressure. I thought of Eliot, the nurse, and his two big tattoo-covered arms.

"Bud, you just got some bad news. Your body is trying to put it in the deep freeze so you don't have to feel it. It's okay, but

I want you to try not to let the sadness become a block of ice." Daniel watched my lips as I talked. "Did you see how Lucy's sadness just popped right out and spilled over? Your sadness is going to need to come out of you too. When you feel it melting and spilling over, can you try and let it out? Promise me?"

I looked at Daniel, just barely younger than I was when we lost Chris—so impossibly and devastatingly small. I thought of the adults who had been younger than I was now. Daniel nodded; his ridiculously blue eyes, heavy with dark lashes, stared earnestly into mine.

"Want to read a book? I'll keep you company?" He nodded again. He pulled a favorite off his shelf and slipped under his sheet.

"I will read to *you*, Mommy." It was the most comfort I'd allowed myself to be offered since coming home.

He picked *Whistle for Willie* by Ezra Jack Keats and read aloud about a little boy named Peter trying to learn to whistle to his dog named Willy. Though he knew the book by heart, he read carefully, being sure not to miss a single word. "He went into his house and put on his father's old hat to make himself feel more grown-up...."

My father had started wearing hats during his chemo.

Daniel's lip quivered. He stopped reading and looked up at me with panic in his eyes.

"It's spilling out, Mommy!" He scrambled into my lap and clutched me in a terrified hug. He let out the loudest sobs I've ever heard from him. I rubbed his back and soothed him with the same shushing I'd used when he was a baby. I held him for an hour at least, until long after numbness had crept down both of my legs. When his breathing evened, I coaxed him back under the covers, rubbing his face gently with the back of my fingers. At nearly midnight, exhaustion blanketed us both.

"Mommy?" he whispered. I shushed him again. "Does cancer always win?"

"No, baby."

"Well, for me it does, one hundred percent." He yawned and rolled his small body away from me toward the wall. It was such a Daniel thought, his mind always organized by math. His memory slipped my father's death into a file alongside his friend from kindergarten.

The house was silent as I poured myself down the stairs. I anticipated finding my husband on the couch, waiting for me.

"Mike?" I called out in the empty quiet.

"Just a second." He was in the office just off the living room. I walked around the couch and caught the weight of three devastated children still imprinted in the fabric. I sank down into the pillows and pulled out my phone, where I found several loving texts from friends and siblings wishing me well with the terrible job of the now broken news. My eyes dipped with the real-life heaviness of it all. When I looked up at the clock, seven minutes had passed.

And I exploded as though I'd been slapped. I streaked into the office where Mike was hunched over his computer, completely engrossed in the screen. "Sorry, I'll be right there," he said casually, not even looking up.

"WHAT THE FUCK ARE YOU DOING?"

Mike's head snapped to attention.

"MY DAD JUST FUCKING DIED!"

He shook his head as if shaking off a trance.

"Of course…"

"AND I JUST COAXED OUR SON INTO CRYING SO HE WON'T BE TRAUMATIZED LIKE I WAS AND YOU THINK I SHOULD WAIT A FEW MORE MINUTES? FOR YOU? WHAT THE FUCK AM I EVEN WAITING FOR?"

I hated him. I felt consumed by it.

"Get the FUCK OUT." I spat the words in his stunned face.

Mike looked at me with genuine fear. He stood up quickly and rushed toward me.

"GET THE FUCK OUT!" I repeated. I immediately understood the sense of betrayal that drives a spouse to change the locks.

"What is the point of you, anyway?" I ran with my rage down into the basement, where we occasionally hosted guests on an old and uncomfortable couch.

"Meghan, wait. I don't want to leave." Some unfamiliar part of me felt relieved at the sound of his fear.

"Well, I *do* want you to leave. I don't *need* you. I've done this completely on my own. I don't need you now. Get your FUCK-ING COMPUTER and GET OUT," I growled like an animal.

Mike feigned defeat and made a movement toward the stairs, but at the last minute he stepped to me and pulled me hard into a hug that I fought against.

"Get off. I don't want you. What the FUCK IS WRONG WITH YOU? My dad DIED. He died. HE DIED. You're fucking *working* and he *died*." I collapsed onto the floor with Mike still clinging to me as my own sadness spilled out over everything. The insult that earth continued to spin without my father on it was something I desperately wanted to be Mike's fault.

"I'm so sorry, babe. I'm so sorry. I'm so, so sorry. I don't know what I'm doing either. I'm so sorry." He stroked my hair and kissed my head.

"Fuck you."

I woke in the morning, physically and emotionally stiff. I felt convinced I'd spent the night shouting at myself rather than at Mike. I despised myself for believing I could depend on him. After a childhood spent refusing to need people and another decade trying to unlearn that lesson, I was stunned to find myself covered in a familiar kind of shame. My old beliefs had found a crack and were successfully creeping back in. I'd accidentally let myself need someone other than me and was suddenly reminded that it was a dangerous way to navigate the world.

FIFTEEN

It's safe to say a lot must go into a marriage of fifty years.

My mother didn't talk much about her grief after my father's death, and I rarely asked about it directly. Once, when it was just the two of us, she turned to me with wide eyes and asked, "Why can't I remember anything about the week he died?" I was grateful to have an answer to give. I quickly pulled up an image of the brain I kept bookmarked on my phone to use in sessions with clients. I talked her through how the hippocampus, the part of the brain that codes memory, malfunctions in times of extreme stress. Memory formation happens but is fractured. Some details are coded with extra weight, while others are lost as though insignificant.

"Thank you," she told me, wiping away tears. "That really helps." She squeezed my forearm and I let myself believe that I had.

. . .

Two years after my father's death, I mentioned to my mother that Mike planned to travel home to England for a few weeks in the summer with the kids.

I took it as a good sign that she immediately suggested she and I could sneak off on a trip of our own.

For weeks we whispered on the phone like coconspirators. Just the suggestion of travel for the two of us harkened back to a magical week we'd spent on Prince Edward Island, a few years before I was married.

"What about Greece?" I asked, starting with the top of my dream travel list.

My mom was thoughtful before replying, "I think maybe somewhere closer."

A few days later, she suggested Boothbay Harbor, a Maine seaside town she'd heard was lovely. I told her I would take a trip to the end of the driveway if she wanted. My mother's undivided attention was something I'd never really stopped craving. I was grateful to be in a place emotionally where I could allow myself to want to spend time with her.

I had a week on my own in my house first where I ate cheese-and-cracker dinners and did no laundry. The kids were enjoying their grandparents in England, though I heard from Mike that our youngest wasn't sleeping much.

"He's afraid to fall asleep, and when he does, he often startles awake."

I sent my best comforting mom voice bouncing across the time zones, to no avail.

"I'm afraid someone I love is going to die," my son said. He had been repeating the phrase night after night.

The nearby adults assumed Nicky was experiencing separation anxiety, but from my vantage point in our empty house, it didn't feel like the entire explanation. I worried Nicky was unhappy but unable to communicate the reasons why with his limited kid vocabulary.

Two days before my flight to Boston, where I'd meet my mom to drive up to Maine, my sister called me with concerns.

"Mom has a terrible stomach bug. She's been sick for days. She may not even make it to Maine."

My mother had said nothing to me. When I called, I made sure she understood I had inside information.

"We can do this anytime. No biggie." I half entertained the idea of going alone. Five days in a seaside village was too good to waste.

"I'm fine. I'll be there."

I accepted my mother's "fine" and assured my sister that I'd keep a watchful eye and adjust our plans accordingly.

As promised, my mother's car was idling in the Logan Airport arrivals bay when I stepped out into the cool Boston air. Our drive north was uneventful, though my mother kept a bottle of ginger ale and Imodium on hand in the back seat.

We agreed to keep things low-key. She ate a little clear broth in the giant tourist-trap restaurant where we stopped an hour into our drive. She seemed chatty, if not quite herself. We'd both brought books, and the bed-and-breakfast run by two male friends we'd mistaken for a couple, much to their delight, had a lovely view of the harbor. If we never made it past the porch, we agreed we'd still be happy.

Breakfast at the inn included yogurt, which seemed to keep my mom content. The cool calmed her stomach, but she also managed coffee and a fruit cup. It wasn't much, but she'd eaten like a bird for so many years that the small amount hardly registered as problematic.

We took a short drive to a nearby town with art galleries and an old-time soda fountain. My mother didn't get out of the car. "I haven't seen a single funeral home," she noted as we drove back to the inn. I laughingly called her morbid, but she smiled and insisted she was "just being practical."

On our second-to-last day, I left on an early coffee run. I dressed carefully and quietly in the bathroom and was surprised I managed to avoid waking my mother. On impulse before I snuck out, I stood over her tiny body on the single bed tucked in the eave of the old inn. I took my mother in as I had my children as babies. Her face was aged; she was an old lady now. I watched her chest rise and fall.

She had showered but was still lying down when I returned a little over an hour later. She'd had a bad night, she explained. She had sweat through her pajamas and had terrible dreams. She worried when she woke and saw my bed empty.

"For some reason I was frightened I'd actually died," she said. "I thought I must be here alone now. I felt terrible for the poor chambermaid who would discover me." She paused and then her voice filled with mirth. "And then I wondered if she would be accused of murder, like in *Murder, She Wrote.*"

We exploded with laughter. My mother's story seemed excellent to both of us. Most of the staff at the inn was Eastern

European, and over breakfast we added a complicated plotline that included a Russian jewel thief and a smuggling ring. We agreed our story would easily make a bestselling book, maybe even a series.

Later, as we sat in the sun and my mother chatted with one of the many older couples also staying at the B&B, I imagined an additional plot twist: the daughter who'd been traveling with the now dead mother would be devastated by the tragedy. Unable to move on, she'd stay in the community and inevitably fall in love with a local—a bartender maybe. She'd drink through her grief until she got sober and was ready to live her life again.

"Sounds like an excellent TV show. I'd watch that," my mother said. I observed her, as I had a hundred times before, break a gingersnap into quarters and dip it into her tea.

On our final morning in Maine, I drove us back to the airport. My mother did not seem better, nor did she seem particularly worse. She refused my hopeful offer to drive her the whole way home to Cape Cod.

"You need to get back," she said sternly. My mother had a particular tone that had a way of ending conversations.

By the time my flight landed in D.C., my mom had texted that she made it home safely. I tried to quiet any lingering concern, remembering that the kids and I would be up at the Cape for our annual beach vacation in just two days' time.

SIXTEEN

After ten hours of driving, I pulled our minivan into my parents' beach house driveway just after dinnertime. The little house had originally been named "Pandemonium" by the Morse family, a large family like ours, who, in 1928, built a family compound consisting of three houses. They sold the "Big House" and the beach house to my parents in 1992 but kept the third and largest house for another decade before selling it to a family with a penchant for Jet Skis and weekend fireworks displays. My crew generally slept up at the Big House with my parents but spent our days lazing on the deck that surrounded Pandemonium on three sides.

My family's two houses were separated by a marsh complete with cattails and peepers. Despite Pandemonium being a three-room cottage with only one bedroom, I spent one of my favorite summers there bunked up with my younger brother and sister while the Big House received such glamorous renovations as drywall, insulation, and reliable hot water.

By the time my father moved us oceanside, he'd managed to create the financial security he always craved. It took a confluence of features to make my mother's lifelong dream of waking up to the five-o'clock dazzle of sunshine dancing across the ocean a reality. My father relied heavily on a longtime friendship with a realtor who would go on to create a near monopoly on Cape Cod waterfront house sales, and created a mortgage joked about in our family to be so precarious the bank would guarantee it for only a week. The house was exactly the kind that would cause you to look up from the beach and think, *I bet it would be amazing to live there.*

It was. It was a gift I neither deserved nor took for granted.

Mike and I had been bringing the kids to the beach since they were babies. First we stayed for a week, then as the kids' love of the ocean developed, we extended our stay for as long as a month. The joy of seeing my children play alongside the children of friends who'd known me since childhood was something I had never considered.

We arrived at dinnertime, hungry and exhausted, but the kids still insisted I pop the trunk so they could yank their suits from the swim bag to take their first dips of the season. The early-evening swim called for culinary simplicity. I texted my mom to ask if she could please bring down a box of pasta and a jar of tomato sauce.

The boys were fully submerged on the sandbar when I was

stunned by the sight of my mother's car pulling up the sandy driveway. The two houses were so close together, no one ever drove. It had been only two days since I'd seen her, but as she stepped out of the car, I noticed my mother's ashen pallor and newly unsteady gait.

"You don't look good." I hugged her gently. I could feel my mother's tiny bones through her thin sweater. She shook her head quickly as if to shake off my comment and waved hello to the kids. Then she sat gingerly in a deck chair. I sat down next to her in silence, trying to make sense of the buzzing in my chest.

"I really don't feel well at all," she said, breaking the silence but still staring out at the sea. My body tingled with truth.

For the next few days, I balanced the kids' needs with checking in on my mom. When I asked her how she was feeling, she'd answer simply, "Not great," but she still managed a run to the grocery store that yielded two six-packs of Italian ice and twelve diet strawberry yogurts.

When Mike flew in three days later, my mother had all but stopped eating. She'd also become vaguer about her symptoms.

"Did you sleep?" I asked.

"I slept," she said, elongating the word in such a way that made it sound as if she really hadn't.

"What about eating?"

"I had a yogurt," she said, again ducking my question behind a thin veil of irritation. I checked the refrigerator daily to confirm that at least one yogurt went missing. When I went to the store, I picked up a jar of organic bone broth for the stupid price of sixteen dollars and pleaded with her to at least try to eat it with an egg.

"You need the protein, Mom," I implored.

"I'll try" was the closest thing to a promise as I was going to get.

On the fifth morning of our vacation, I woke early, terrified by the stillness coming from her bedroom. I waited a beat, and, in what played out like a dress rehearsal for what was to come, I knocked. I turned the handle quickly, expecting to see my mother collapsed on the floor. Instead, I found an unmade bed—another clue of the degree of her illness—and an empty room. I discovered her lying on the chaise on the first floor. My panic was still high.

"I think you need to let me take you to a doctor."

"It's just a stomach bug." I could tell her heart wasn't in it.

"Listen, I just opened the door of your bedroom . . ." My voice trailed off.

"You are supposed to be on vacation," she offered, as if illness kept to a calendar.

I gave her a head tilt and an annoyed, incredulous look I'd learned at her knee.

I tried logic, stressing that it made sense to let me take her when neither Mike nor I had work calls and he could easily manage the kids.

"Okay, Meg," she said softly. She sounded as if she might cry.

I was familiar with the partially refrigerated feel of hospitals, so I stuffed a pair of socks and a sweater for my mother into my bag before we left the house. We didn't wait long in the ER, and when we were taken to an exam room, a doctor immediately ordered an IV. I offered my mom the socks and sweater, but instead she asked for her rosary. My mother and I had both spent many hours standing around a hospital bed the last year of my father's life. I saw her wipe away a few tears, but, for her sake, pretended I hadn't.

Once the IV was in, my mother quickly began to improve. The pink returned to her skin, and her body notably softened. "Okay, you're right. I'm freezing," she said with a giggle.

I rummaged quickly through my bag but found only the sweater. Without stopping to think, I surreptitiously slipped my feet out of my sneakers, stepped on the toes of my socks, and, one after the other, tugged them off.

My mother pulled the tiny cotton sweater up over her arms like a toddler, but only as far as the IV permitted. I moved to the end of her gurney and carefully slipped her child-sized, icy feet into my still warm socks. She looked down at the mismatched athletic logos and wiggled her toes in satisfaction.

After a minute she said, "Can I ask you a question?"

I nodded.

"Did you take these socks off *your* feet?"

I gave her a smart-ass "Yep."

She pursed her lips.

"Can I ask you another question?'

I grinned. I knew.

"Why don't young people care if their socks match these days? It's ridiculous."

"Woman, just shut up and say thank you."

She reached over and squeezed my hand.

Ultimately an ultrasound gave no indication of the root cause of her illness. Rosier, brighter, and physically less tense, my mother was released with the instruction to follow up with her primary-care doctor.

"I was just so afraid they were going to tell me I had stomach cancer," she said, then exhaled. "I didn't realize how much my body was hurting."

For some reason, neither of us wondered *why* she felt better or worried that her pain would inevitably return.

In the car on the way home from the hospital my mother teared up a bit.

"I really appreciate this, you know." I remembered that without my father, my mother had no one to cajole or boss her into getting help.

"I know, Mommy. Thank you for letting me take you."

For the few hours her face glowed healthy and pain-free, my mother managed to eat an entire yogurt cup, and we allowed ourselves to hope we were on the right side of time.

Two days after our trip to the ER, my mother drove herself to a follow-up appointment with her regular doctor. She reported back that she'd been instructed to cut out dairy. I asked gentle questions when I saw her meager meals change from yogurt to store-bought Italian ice, made only of sugar and water. My mother insisted I defer to her interpretation of her doctor's orders. Her rings spun on her already tiny fingers.

I tried to walk the delicate edge of being helpful versus being an intrusive bully. My mother's privacy lines had always been much more well defined than mine. Every day I would

END OF THE HOUR

ask if she felt any better and she'd shake her head no. I followed up, hoping she would let me again take her to the doctor, but did not insist. Once, she unexpectedly met my fear with anger.

"Don't go making appointments behind my back," she snapped, in what I assumed was a reference to the care I'd provided my father before he died.

"When have I ever done that? How about you don't *make* me call the doctor."

"Don't you dare." Her voice was filled with disdain.

A medical minimizer her whole life, it would be months before it occurred to me she was likely in much more pain than she ever let on. As a clinician, I knew a high pain tolerance is often found in trauma survivors, though I never realized that also included my mother. She pushed away my help and succeeded in hurting me just enough that I kept even more of a distance between us for the next few days.

SEVENTEEN

The ocean is stunning at all times of day, but the fives are my favorite. At 5:00 p.m., the sun on the beach grass glows a watercolor sort of gold. I always planned my summer evenings around trying to catch it. At 5:00 a.m., the sun yawns awake and stretches long pink streaks of light across the horizon. Small puffs of air dance across the still, glassy surface of the ocean, and the sea rolls in dappled light.

"Diamonds on the water," my mother always said.

It took only a few days at the Cape for my kids to settle into their favorite summer activities—beach walks, swimming, and daily trips to the ice-cream shack. On our sixth day, I woke to a red sunrise and a silent house. I took advantage of the quiet by sneaking down to the beach.

I stepped onto the deck of the beach house and took in a glimpse of Martha's Vineyard on the horizon. With one deep sigh, I settled myself into a lounger with my book. When a fishing boat eased to the required "slow, no-wake" speed of five miles per hour through the channel, I didn't even bother to look up. But it was in the whine of the disappearing boat motor that I heard someone yell, "HELP!"

The cry was distinguishable immediately. I popped up like a gopher, as if I'd expected it. Despite all my therapy, I was still a child of trauma, hyperalert even as I tried to relax.

"Help!"

Suddenly, I was running and yelling.

I ran toward our red sea kayak resting in the shrubs. I couldn't actually carry the boat myself, but somehow I *did*. There was a third call, then a fourth, but there wasn't a fifth.

In the echoing silence, my past and present melded together, and suddenly I was not just paddling toward a man in distress, I was racing to rescue a little girl who'd accidentally played a helpless part in a drowning on this same shoreline decades ago.

"WHERE IS HE? WHERE IS HE?" I screamed to no one.

Rapidly skimming down the water's edge, I saw a set of arms flailing on the shore in the distance. I paddled with the fast-moving current and heard the woman call to me, "He's here! He's here!"

"Is his head above water? Why can't I hear him?" I felt hope slipping away as my voice and body shook.

My eyes scanned to where the woman pointed far in the distance. I had to squint before I could just barely see the man's head. I couldn't tell if he was face up or moving.

"Please, please, please, please, please," I pleaded to no one and nothing in particular. "This can't be my story again."

Finally, the man turned his head to me. I was out of breath and could barely move my arms, but my body exploded in relief.

"Are you okay?" he asked me.

"Am *I* okay?" I was utterly confused.

"*I'm* all right," he said. There was a tone in his voice I couldn't quite place. "I'm just doing some arm exercises."

I was completely incredulous.

"YOU YELLED 'HELP!'"

"Oh, I'm sorry," he said, sounding not the least bit sorry. "I was just yelling at the boat. I thought I'd get a tow back in, but really, I'm fine."

I turned my tears away from the swimmer, wondering how on earth my panic to save a stranger had landed me cloaked in shame. Overreaction is also a trauma response that, for me, often came with a light dusting of humiliation.

I noted a policeman waving from the beach. My co-rescuer was now in the water, swimming toward us.

"Apparently, we're fine," I yelled, hoping my voice made it to the shore.

"I'm Tim. What's your name, hon? I'm sorry I scared you and your friend." The swimmer's voice sounded warmer.

"I'm Meghan. And that's just another woman who thought you needed saving." I pointed toward the swimmer moving toward us.

"My son's wife's name is Meghan; they live in West Bridge-water," Tim offered, apropos of nothing.

The woman swam up to us. My shoulders unlocked in the immediate relief of her presence. She seemed unfazed by the much ado about nothing.

"I'm Kate." She flashed me a big smile and turned to the man. "You don't look so good," she said to Tim.

I hadn't noticed, but Kate was right. Tim was the same gray I'd recently seen on my mother.

"Take the towline, Tim," I said firmly. "Since we have an audience now, how about you let me feel like a hero and paddle you in?" A few beachcombers had joined the policeman at the water's edge.

"What's your name, hon?" Tim asked me again.

I raised an eyebrow to Kate. "I'm Meghan, and that's Kate."

"I have a son named Meghan..." Tim's voice trailed off.

"Hey, Tim. Can you take the rope, please?" Kate's voice reminded me of an ER nurse I'd worked with years ago, gentle but firm. Shame washed over me again, this time in the relief that I hadn't been wrong to panic.

Moments later, Tim was barking out orders. "Paddle on the left. You need to paddle harder or we won't get anywhere."

"Fuck you, Tim," I mumbled under my breath. My anger always showed up as an emotional bouncer for my fear.

A fire-and-rescue boat sped up alongside us. The crew spoke firmly to Tim, telling him to climb the ladder into the boat. Kate and I locked eyes and listened as the crew behind us discovered Tim's arm had seized up and wouldn't unlock.

"He didn't even say thank you," Kate said, panting as we pulled ourselves out of the water a half hour later. The policeman who greeted us explained they had discovered Tim's shoes miles down the beach. It was barely six o'clock, and he had been in the water for at least an hour when we found him. He was taken to the hospital disoriented, but safe.

When I sat on the edge of my mother's chaise a few hours later, I tried to retell the story of the rescue. My words evaporated when I got to the part when I could no longer hear Tim's voice. I felt myself pulled back into the sense memory of bodily terror when it seemed that I was paddling toward death.

"But what in the world made you think to get the boat?" my mother asked. I couldn't tell whether she sounded impressed or irritated.

"I didn't think," I replied honestly. I knew trauma often immobilizes a person. I was just glad mine had picked movement—fight over freeze this time around.

I might have been thirty-six years late, but I'd never stop rushing to that little nine-year-old girl who hoped there might still be a chance of rescue.

EIGHTEEN

Since taking my mother to the hospital, I had increasingly avoided both her illness and her irritation. I planned a whale-watching tour with friends even though I was 100 percent aware this choice would put me on the water for six hours with no cell signal and no way to help her if something happened. I had friends in town who had never seen whales. I told myself I was being a gracious hostess, but I felt more like a child eager for distraction. Later, I would wonder what I thought I was distracting myself from.

Before I left for the day, my mother told me not to worry. "I'll call the church ladies if I need anything." She never would have asked me to not go.

When I blew her a kiss goodbye as she lay on her favorite chair, I did so as her daughter. Countless times since, I've wished I acted more like a clinician.

In the days to come, the toggle between *I couldn't have known* and *I should have known* would batter me relentlessly.

I wish I'd thought to check if she was steady on her feet. I wish I'd asked if her pain was worse. I could have assessed the quality of her decision-making by coyly asking a few questions from the mental status exam. I did not ask what she last ate or how much water she'd had.

Instead, I teased her that our "asshole" puppy would keep her company.

She laughed. "Get that fucking dog away from me."

Those were the last words my mother ever said to me.

It was not until her funeral that I learned the moment I walked out the door, she got up and drove herself to the house of her friend, a monsignor, a mile away, where she requested a "blessing of the sick." I wasn't surprised to hear she'd driven, though I'd forbidden it. My mother was incredibly strong-willed, and I was grateful for it in the end. Though my denial had me floating as far away from my mother's death as I could get, I understood that she found her own way to drive toward it.

Back late from our boat trip, I asked Mike to drop me at our friends' house and then swing around to check on my mother while I helped start dinner. Still feeling the tension of a middle place between her and me, it seemed safer to send him. If my mother was awake, she and Mike would be easier on each other.

He returned minutes later with the report he'd driven up the driveway and right back down after he saw her bedroom light was already out.

Unaware of what the following day would ask of us, Mike pulled up his chair to a table full of our friends. He and I clinked cold glasses of wine over steaming bowls of seafood. Someone casually mentioned a prediction of rain for the morning, and I stupidly promised a week of relentless sunshine.

NINETEEN

I drove an hour and seventeen minutes through careful desperation to be with my mother's body after she died.

I'd left the house with the kids the next morning to go to Boston to pick up my best friend Maia's son and bring him back to the beach with us for a few days. It rained lightly the whole way. Like marauding pirates after rumored treasure, my kids tumbled out of our minivan practically before it came to a full stop. They scrambled up the wooden stairs to grab their "cousin" while I sat alone in the driver's seat.

I watched misty droplets collect on the windshield as my mind wandered. Suddenly, I felt an acute internal contraction from my pelvis, like a phantom "water breaking." The sensation seized me from deep inside and felt so real, I looked down at my legs expecting to see wetness. Like cold air on a subzero New England day, my mind froze with one crystalized thought.

She's dead.

My body told me, and I knew it was true.

I scrambled to call my mother's house and was not surprised when the phone rang four times before going to voice mail.

I couldn't unknow what I knew.

I texted my husband, who was working back at the house: *Have you seen my mom today?*

I started the engine like a getaway driver and yelled at the kids to hurry as they stepped on each other's feet climbing back inside the minivan.

Mike texted back: *Maybe a friend picked her up for morning Mass?*

The idea was so ludicrously out of step with the frail woman we'd visited with for only minutes the day before. I started driving.

Mike texted again: *Her bedroom door is still closed. Do you want me to go in?*

In only a matter of moments, we'd found ourselves at the threshold every griever knows—the precipice of before and after. Survivors of untenable loss relive one moment of their lives a thousand times over; this one would become mine. My efforts to stay planted in my "before" were no match for the inevitability of time. I felt panic rise as I texted my reply: *I need you to go in. Please. I'm sorry.*

I understood the cost of my ask.

A hundred thousand lifetimes of seconds went by, but also less than five minutes.

I called Mike. It went to voice mail, and I knew he was on the phone with paramedics. The car clock said the time was 10:28 a.m. I marked the moment the world was lost to me.

Fumbling to drive and text, I somehow also took a screenshot of my phone. Months later I would find the odd photographic documentation of my devastation.

"Mom?" Lucy's voice was tentative and questioning from the passenger seat. We both kept our eyes trained on the road in front of us. Out of the corner of my mind I could see her face flushed with fear. I exhaled in an effort to keep my composure. "I think we are about to get some really bad news, honey," I said.

I will remember the grace of my eleven-year-old daughter's reply for the rest of my life. She did not ask me to explain but instead offered simply, "Do you want me to help you?"

My forty-five-year-old nine-year-old self said: "Yes, please. Yes."

Lucy reached over and put her hand on the steering wheel, firmly covering mine.

"We are going to box-breathe. Can you do that? Do you want me to count for you?" Her voice was soft but controlled. I'd taught her the meditative practice of box breathing after she saw a scary movie at a friend's house and had a few nights of troubled sleep. The breath calms the body while the instructions distract the mind.

I nodded.

Lucy drew a horizontal line in the air. "Deep breath in for four." Vertical line down. "Hold for four." Horizontal line across. "Exhale for four." Vertical line up. "Pause for four." Her voice was rhythmic. "Deep breath in for four, hold for four, exhale for four, pause for four." Seven minutes of breathing; a gift from a daughter to a mother.

Two thousand years and seven minutes later, my phone rang, and the man who would do anything for me, including this, told me to find a place to pull over. It struck me as a bizarre formality of safety at a time when the world no longer tilted correctly on its axis, but his voice shook, and he insisted. I followed my husband's instructions and pulled onto a cloverleaf exit, which led me to a large, long abandoned parking lot with a decrepit off-brand Dairy Queen in the far corner.

I immediately called Mike back. "Tell me. Say it."

His voice cracked with emotion. I floated slightly out of my body, observing the impossibility of the moment. Somehow, I still had the presence of mind to walk around the side of the ice-cream hut to hide my body language from the kids.

"I'm so sorry, honey." He didn't really have to say it after all.

"Oh my God. She died." I said it for us. Then, as if to double-check, I asked it as a question. "She really died?"

"I'm so sorry, babe." It was the best he had and the most he could give me in that moment.

I felt the physical duality of what happened next. Like inhaling noxious gas, I noted the exact second when my mind began to turn on me. I heard my own corruption of thought: "It's just such a terrible consequence..."

"What is, baby?"

I did not complete the sentence, but the idea had formed in titanium: *I did not do enough. It's my fault she died.*

I unexpectedly felt my torso yanked violently up with the force and momentum of a careening roller coaster. In a moment both predestined and utterly out of control, my body crested into a blissful kind of weightlessness. For three glorious seconds, I felt a sensation best described as excitement. It reminded me of the time I watched a murmuration of black starlings swirl and pulse across an evening sky. My mother was dead, and my body felt thrilled.

It wasn't the first time I felt this duality.

I'd had a client once describe the exact sensation to me. Like him, I'd carried shame that my body's experience of some of the worst moments of my life was a sensation of joy.

"I'd just heard the worst news possible," he confessed to me, sobbing, "and instead of feeling heartbroken I felt..." His voice trailed off.

"Excited. Thrilled," I said, finishing his sentence for him.

My client's eyes widened with shock, and my stomach lurched in the truth that most people never speak aloud. We sat for a few moments saying nothing.

I was able to give my client the same explanation I had been given by a neuroscientist once when I wasn't even looking for it. She'd explained that the brain sends adrenaline, like a security detail racing across the body, determined to create an energetic cushion of protection from the impending trauma. What felt like excitement was really the body's defense system of flooding itself with the neurotransmitter adrenaline.

When my mother experienced a similar sensation while holding her own ninety-nine-year-old dying mother's hand, I tried to offer her the same science to explain her self-described "surge of overwhelming peace and love."

"Maybe, Meg," she replied gently after I gave my quick and basic lecture, "but I'm pretty sure what I felt was just God."

Standing in the parking lot with Mike's breathy voice still

on the other side of the line, I did not feel God. I did not even feel science. Instead, I felt the fear of a nine-year-old girl who had, somehow, discovered herself completely alone once again.

Like a children's game of telephone gone awry, I immediately understood just how wrong Elisabeth Kübler-Ross was with her five stages of grief. There was no anger, no denial, no bargaining, no time for depression—only acceptance existed. My body had declared my mother's death. My husband had confirmed it. The only thing left was the loss of her and how I would try to face that.

Just as it had in my childhood, my mind insisted the emotions currently overwhelming me were not just what I felt, they were who I was—a self-centered, distracted, and crappy daughter who'd used my mother for her beach house. I couldn't have been bothered to stop vacationing long enough to check in on her health. I didn't care enough to tend to my mother, and she died. I would carry the pain of it for the rest of my life.

That guilt felt like a first responder rushing to rescue me from the utter destruction of my life. It offered me an endless loop to busy my mind. I could circle the familiar thought track of "It's my fault" for hours and days rather than attempt to bushwhack my way through the terrifying wilderness of a new life without my mother.

I immediately called all five of my siblings from the parking lot. Nearly a year later, it would occur to me that I could have called their partners. I could have ensured the news of our mother's death was delivered in person by someone they loved.

When the idea found me, I had to work hard not to add it to the list of things for which I could not forgive myself.

"It's my fault," I said in each call. I was desperate to confess and answer for my crimes. In the moment my clarity of thinking was not sharp enough to recall that trauma survivors often hold themselves accountable for the terrible thing rather than accepting that they couldn't have prevented it.

I cannot remember most of what was said to my siblings, only that I felt myself crumbling. One brother spoke to me with an intolerable, gentle patience that left me desperate to get off the phone. My little sister was firm and insistent that I should not blame myself, while my older sister screamed and accidentally hung up on me. I know I heard each one say, "This is not your fault." Like black mold, my corruption of culpability grew quickly, finding all my darkest places that had remained damp with fear and shame since childhood.

After my last call, I pressed my face against the bricks of the building where I hid. They were caked in car exhaust. Out of the corner of my eye I noticed my foot in my well-worn Birkenstock. A chipped pedicured toenail peeked out. How long had it been since I painted my nails? My thoughts were nonsensical, but I couldn't stop my mind from trying to pull me from the brutal present.

When I called Maia, I feared she would ask me to turn around and drop her son back home. As if that was something anyone would have expected of me in that moment. Instead, she asked multiple times if she could come get me. I could just drop a pin on my GPS and wait for her.

I imagine I appeared and sounded calm, but I needed to

keep moving. Like a shark swimming to stay alive, I felt my focus narrow on my target. "I need to get to her. I can't wait here." Maia didn't fight. It was hard to know whose love felt more powerless in that moment.

I paused before climbing back inside the car. In a violent internal tug-of-war, I had brutal clarity regarding the choice that needed to be made. I had to pick; it was me or the kids. I could not be my mother's daughter, utterly destroyed, in this exact moment and also be the mother responsible for getting these children home. I brushed aside the shadow of my broken self and chose the idling minivan full of kids over my own cascading sadness. It took only a moment to zip myself back inside myself. I'd had practice, after all.

I watched my cell phone die, reached for a charger cord that wasn't there, and realized I had only myself to rely on for the next hour. In the coming months, I'd return to this moment a thousand times and wonder: *If I had asked for help at the time, what might it have saved me from later?*

"Daddy is with Nana, and I have to get to them," I lied to Lucy as I started up the car.

"Is everything okay?" she asked in a far-too-grown-up voice.

"We are okay." Like a war of semantics or slick legalese, everything I said was technically true.

I felt my trauma therapist's mind sharpen. I began to coach myself as I would a patient, to look around and find handrails to steady myself. Over Lucy's protests, I clicked off the radio. No music to make an associative trigger. How many stories had I heard where a particular song caused floods of tears in a grocery store? Mercifully, Lucy filled the silence by reciting the comprehensive list of school supplies she would need when classes started back in a few weeks.

When newly minted therapists find themselves unexpectedly flooded by emotion on account of something a client says, we teach them the session-saving skill of "mirroring." It's the simple and effective tool of actively listening by repeating back every word a client says. It sounds too ridiculously simple, but it works, especially with the highly distressed, who, more than anything, need to feel heard. I mirrored Lucy for the entire hour and seventeen minutes, until I made it back home to be with my mother's body.

TWENTY

When I finally stood over the place where my mother's life had laid itself down, I desperately needed to honor her in the way she would have wanted, the way she would have attended to her people. I told Mike I needed to go in to see her alone.

Her tiny body was barely a lump under the pale blue bedcover. Equally drawn in and repelled, my feet danced a double step at the threshold before I managed to coax myself to kneel at her bedside. I brushed my hand across the large silver rosary still wrapped around her slightly bluish fingers. I asked Mike, whom I felt hovering on the other side of the bedroom door, to find me another rosary. I pushed her curls from her face and fully closed her eyes, just like people do in the movies.

"I'm so sorry, Mommy. I'm so sorry," I whispered. I felt a pain like a hand clutching my lungs and twisting. For a moment, like hers, my breath stopped.

Mike knocked before he tiptoed in with multiple strands of brightly colored plastic beads looped over his forearm like a one-person Mardi Gras. More than once in the week leading up to her death, my mother said, "Just hand me a rosary, Meg." I was unsure whether she offered prayers for others or for herself, but I knew she deserved them from me now. Fragments of the rituals of her faith floated in my memory.

My phone shook in my left hand as Google gifted me with the familiar image of a small rosary instructional card. I again tried to pin my mind to the present moment but found it wandering too powerfully at the sight of the picture on the screen.

My grandmother, my mother's mother, had given me a white patent leather Bible with the same instructional card when I made my First Communion on the still innocent side of eight. She'd had my name embossed on the cover in gold letters. I adored my grandmother, but I never managed to open her precious book with its onionskin pages. As an adult I was pretty sure I had felt something like "God" on occasion. But in times of need or sorrow, I hedged my bets and asked my mother to activate her "church ladies" prayer chain. "Okay, Meg," she'd say. "We're on it." The grace of her faith had always extended to all of us.

Now staring at her lifeless hand, I rolled a rosary bead between my thumb and first two fingers. I felt the imprint of her worry and prayer-filled hours pressed into the cut plastic sphere. Panic filled my chest. Every minute I wasn't saying the rosary, I felt I was failing her. I was acutely aware it wasn't the first time.

As I had done during the many grade school holiday concerts my mother attended, I gave an overly enthusiastic, amateur performance. Awkwardly switching my weight from knee to knee, stopping and starting, I was desperate to anoint my mother's body in her beloved and sacred prayers. If I had hoped for spiritual grace, it had not found me.

Months later, I would think back to this sorrow-filled moment and see it as a gift to both my mother and me. I'd spent half my lifetime seeking spiritual connection through the rituals she, and those of other faiths, so loved. My mother had wanted the rosary to offer me help and healing. I am certain she would have been grateful that I found myself greeting her death on my knees in prayer.

I clicked the instruction photo on my phone: one bead of the Our Father and ten Hail Marys. I recalled both prayers easily. The Glory Be was short but utterly forgotten, and—hand to God—I'd never seen or heard the Hail Holy Queen or the Mysteries before in my life. It took nearly thirty minutes before I awkwardly traced my fingers down to the cross.

I stood, and my hands opened themselves stiff and flat. I pressed down on the bed gingerly, the way you test a burner for heat. I pressed my palms softly on her tiny, still body. I pressed her prayers and my love into her flesh in the last laying of hands.

I moved slowly through her room, pressing my palms across every surface, honoring her, memorizing her, holding her things, and drawing the remnants of her life out of them and back into me.

· · ·

Two hours later, my brother sat at the end of her bed. By then I had tucked the blue of my mother's hands and feet back inside the covers, pulling the blanket up to her chin.

"She looks so peaceful, just like she's sleeping," he said through his tears.

The solace my brother found instantly and effortlessly had not found me. I couldn't have known it yet, but the images of my mother's well-anointed body would soon haunt me like specters intent on my destruction.

Complex trauma can develop when a person who has experienced past trauma lingers again in fear without support or relief. Compound trauma can occur when more than one overwhelmingly bad thing happens in a short span of time. Weeks from now, I would rage in stunned disappointment that my decades of study and clinical practice failed to act as a forcefield of safety around me. Instead, my mind became thoroughly corrupted by relentless thoughts and images born of the hours I spent alone, trying to serve my mother by neglecting myself.

TWENTY-ONE

It took a few days before my five siblings and I could finally gather together in my mother's kitchen. We spent the early part of the week checking off the many tasks a death and a funeral require. We opened her doors to friends from far and wide as they began showing up with food, kids, and dogs. They hugged and consoled us, offering various memories that left us in tears of laughter and appreciation.

Inevitably, the funeral home called with a deadline. If we wanted time to alert people of my mother's funeral Mass, we had exactly one hour to submit her obituary to the paper.

"I don't feel good about this," I said out loud. I know people heard me.

Because her funeral was still several days away, my siblings piled into their cars to go back to nearby houses or to the homes of loving friends on nearby islands. My younger sister and I found ourselves alone in front of a blinking computer cursor and a clock running out.

My brother had helped by starting to write: "Riordan, Mary F., loving wife, mother, and grandmother, passed away on Tuesday, August 13, 2019, at her home in Cotuit, MA. She was seventy-five. Mary was preceded in death by her husband, John T. Riordan. She is survived by her six children...."

My fingers clicked rapidly over the keys. Luckily, Mike and I had given my father an early eightieth birthday present just after his cancer diagnosis—a biographer hired to write his life story. In an unexpected twist, the editor had managed to get my normally very private mother to talk about herself, and the project had morphed into the story of the life my parents built together. The manuscript was, ironically, left unfinished. I quickly pulled up the file, and my sister and I culled as many details as we could before clicking send with only three minutes to spare.

No one noticed until the next day that one of my brothers had been left off the list of next of kin. I gritted my teeth at the sight of my carelessness in print. The obituary had already been posted on the funeral home's website, and though the neglected brother insisted over email it was "no big deal," it absolutely was. We were only days without my mother, and already it felt like what was left of my family was falling apart.

My reaction was outsized, but I could not stop it. Everything about death feels permanent. I left several messages reflecting my increasing desperation with the paper and the funeral home. Surely, at least one of my mistakes could be fixed. I was in the passenger seat of our car when Amy from the *Cape Cod Times* called back.

"The paper has been put to bed." From her voice, I could tell Amy was older, possibly old enough to have clout.

"Please, you don't understand. This can't be what gets printed. Her children were the thing that mattered most to her." I waved to Mike to pull over and stepped out onto the grassy median.

"It's not possible, I'm so sorry," Amy said. She did sound sorry.

"Amy, do you have siblings? Are your parents alive? Can you imagine how you would feel if you were left out of an obituary? Can you imagine the meaning you might take away from this mistake? I am begging you. This will destroy me. Please. I know you can do something." I felt the familiar blend of anger and panic bubbling in my chest. Hadn't I pleaded like this with doctors and social workers when my father was dying? Bargaining was one of Kübler-Ross's defunct stages; maybe begging was one of mine.

My desperation to mitigate some part of our collective pain reverberated across the cell signal. Amy's pause told me she was going to try to help, and I immediately began to weep.

"Give me a second." Amy kept me on hold for several minutes before she came back.

"Okay, spell the name."

I got back in the car. "We are never telling this story to anyone," I told my husband, as if a secret could ever be the net that catches you or keeps you safe.

TWENTY-TWO

For the next several days, I functioned almost like a child's toy, so wound up I was afraid I'd grind to a permanent halt if I allowed myself to stop moving. I occasionally experienced a confusing sort of déjà vu, which I attributed to the close timing of my parents' deaths. I sent a thank-you text to a friend for a grief book she had given me when my father died two years prior. I had a dizzying moment with the gentleman from the funeral home when he held out a handkerchief holding the jewelry my mother had on when she died. I expected to see my father's wedding ring. I took one look at the small nest of bracelets and rings and replied, "Those must be someone else's." My survival strategy became completing tasks. When I ran out of things to keep me busy, I created them.

For a nonexistent reason I became fixated on the need to dispose of my mother's medications. She kept the half dozen mitigators of aging, cholesterol, and blood pressure issues tidily stored in an absurdly small woven basket on her counter. I collected the handful of orange containers with anyone-proof white caps snapped tight and drove alone to the local pharmacy, realizing I had never thought to check if my mother had even been taking her pills.

My father's leftover medicines had been more radioactive. When the hospice workers took one look at the felony amount of opioids I'd convinced *each* of my father's doctors to prescribe, they insisted first on a pill safe, then on witnessing us destroy the pills by grinding them into coffee grounds hours after he died.

I once helped a worried client dispose of more than five thousand pills she'd discovered after the death of a loved one. No addiction or ill intent, just an old lady who spent a lifetime refilling prescriptions as fast as she forgot to take them. Once at the pharmacy, I knew to ask about the medication mail-back program that manufacturers offered to assure chemicals were properly destroyed. The prepaid envelopes were available wherever prescriptions were filled.

"Oh, we don't do that anymore," the pharmacist with the eyes and the cowlick of a boy I once babysat said flatly.

He pointed instead to a large metal mailbox affixed to the wall. The graphics and signage clearly identified it as a pill repository.

"Make sure to pull off the labels," he said, smiling with familiar dimples, and added meaningfully, "for privacy."

For reasons I can't explain, I couldn't pivot. I'd expected a passive, hermetically sealed experience, but this process required me to face that in her illness, my mother may have made herself sicker by missing medicines. It was yet another thing I could have perhaps prevented by being more attentive.

I tried not to panic.

This is not a problem. It's just different. I used the long-ago mantra given to me by a therapist whose name I couldn't recall. I chanted to myself for several minutes.

This is not a problem. It's just different.

This is not a problem. It's just different.

For a moment, I fixated on a small fire extinguisher, just in my eyeline. "In case of fire, break glass." I felt like I might be the glass.

I sucked in air and noticed people noticing me, but I couldn't rein myself in.

This is not a problem. It's just different.

This is not a problem. It's just different.

A grandmother-type woman stepped up to my left elbow. Our shoulders parallel, she wordlessly and gently pried the container from my hand.

Still facing forward, she popped the top with the force of habit and sluiced the stream of small oblong pills down the long metal chute. She wrapped her hands tightly around the cylinder, her knobby knuckles protruding, and used the ridges of her yellowing nail to scratch off the label. The bottle soon slid to be reunited with its medicine, and she grabbed and gripped another pill case, beginning the process again. I took a breath and followed her lead like a mother instructing her young. Several more rain-stick showers of pellet-sized chemicals down into the box, and we were finished.

The older woman turned swiftly and hugged me. Though she was half my size, she held all my weight.

I gasped—just one childlike sob into her cotton-candy hair. We pulled apart and she gave my arm a reassuring pinch.

I turned toward the pharmacist. I was desperate to leave, but I couldn't. *Andy.* My memory gave me his name as a gift. As a four-year-old, he loved applesauce and took naps holding his favorite cherry-red Matchbox car.

His name tag declared he was "Anderson" now. It was then that I asked him the world's most unfair question.

"Would she have died if she forgot any of those pills?"

I couldn't tell if he also recognized me, but he asked for my mother's birthdate and gave me an answer anyway.

"No. None of those medicines were life-sustaining. I can't tell you why she died, but it wasn't that." Andy gave me a taut, compassionate smile.

My relief lasted only a minute. I needed to blame myself. Blame distracted me from the terrifying idea that death is a dictator. It does not collaborate. It does what it likes. Like a deranged emotional vending machine, my mind quickly dispensed another version of blame to ruminate on: the killer wasn't a lack of medication but instead a lack of medical intervention. I did not thoroughly examine my mother's symptoms, despite being the closest thing my family has to a member of the medical field. This new thought had a longer shelf life and would go on to torture me off and on for years.

Unlike after my father's death, my siblings and I had no long list of people to notify. Each day one of us would text another with the name of an additional person we'd just realized would need to be alerted. My mother's list of people was also different. Her beloved hairdresser whose son had cancer; the dental technician whose infertility journey she'd followed as though her own child was going through it; and the nurse from our grandmother's memory-care center. They'd kept in touch for over a decade. Each person told a story of something my mother gave—a cross-stitched sampler for a grandchild, a check for a GoFundMe—but it was the entry on the funeral home memorial page written by one of her beloved lawn crew that left us all in tears. He told the story of his first encounter with my mother, who was known for leaving refreshments out for her hardworking gardeners.

The entry read: "We were finishing up, and I saw this little old lady coming down the stairs with a heated plate of food in Tupperware and a 2-liter bottle of lemonade. On the way back to the truck we had no idea what was in the container, and for some reason we guessed chicken wings. We were wrong— warm brownies with hot fudge! I never was able to catch her name that day, so from then on we just referred to her as, 'The Chicken Wing Lady.'"

I could hear my mother retelling the story, pretending to be offended, but she would have actually adored the nickname. As far as I was concerned, those few lines trumped the obituary as a fitting tribute.

My older brother, younger sister, and I went to the funeral home the next morning. From the outside, Chapman, Cole, and Gleason could have easily passed for an old Boston law firm. I had driven by the understated and expensive-looking sign, shaded by a large and healthy oak tree, for a lifetime without ever wondering what the building was like inside.

After some confusion over the parking signs (were we guests or family?), we were greeted under the funeral home's imposing white columns by Jan, who'd also helped organize my father's service. "I'm so sorry for your loss," she said, as if we had simply forgotten where we had put our mother. I hated hearing the phrase, though I couldn't yet imagine how much worse it would feel when people stopped offering us condolences altogether.

The next two hours were surreal. With soft voices and signatures in triplicate, we agreed to dispose of our mother's body for the price of a used car. Jan took us through the urn room, where understated vessels sat next to those with unicorn themes and musical vases painted solid gold. Jan rested her hand on a pink-and-purple container with a frosted glass lid that, from my angle, looked exactly like a breast with a nipple. It was impossible to keep myself from snickering.

My sister tossed a "don't you dare" look over her shoulder, and I suddenly missed my mother with such force that I felt like I'd been punched. I had been inadvertently collecting the day's details in the hopes of hearing her giggle over the inanity later on the phone.

Back in Jan's office I realized this moment was why I had insisted on coming. I could feel the precipice of my self-betrayal. Jan asked, as I knew she had to by law, "What about an autopsy?" Her words were gentle. Though I mostly despised her, I was grateful for the care in her voice.

"No." My siblings said it in unison, two out of three. I knew they would. Who would want to butcher their mother's body looking for answers they didn't need? They had no guilt to assuage. My mind was like a garden full of invasive vines— once guilt got in, its tendrils threatened to take the whole place down.

I was surprised when Jan turned and looked right at me. "And how about you?"

Did Jan know I held myself accountable for my mother's death? Could she see that rather than lessen over time, my guilt would increase with such a wild intensity that I would soon stop sleeping entirely? Could Jan have foreseen that even after impaneling my own group of doctors to review my mother's anecdotal medical information, their conclusion that she likely died of a bleeding ulcer would cause me to invent even more unlikely reasons to implicate myself in her death?

I understood the autopsy could just as easily damn me or set me free. I knew what I needed and wanted and that I would not ask for it.

"I'm okay," I heard myself lie to everyone.

I kept my daily death schedule relentless. Later that afternoon, I took Lucy to visit my mother's group of dear friends from her church's tiny but mighty charity shop. "The League of Old Ladies," as we called them: LOLs for short. I felt that I *should* go, but I also wanted to. The group of sixteen women had worked together every Monday and Thursday for years.

Lucy and I walked through the volunteer entrance all conviction and bravado but collapsed completely when we found her beloved team drinking tea, eating cake, and generally getting on with it.

They swarmed like pigeons when they saw us, pecking us with love and hugs.

"You were so important to my mother," I said, my words suddenly tear-choked.

"We loved her," they said back in their various ways.

Every woman in the room was over seventy and deeply religious, and had no trouble declaring my mother to be "with your father now" or "looking down from heaven." Standing in the church outpost, I found it simple to take in their words as loving morsels, like the crumbs of the muffins—a different kind of Eucharist—that they baked each other every week.

My mother's death was not a tragedy to this group. They made casseroles, sang hymns, buried each other's beloveds and their own adored members week after week, year after year, ad infinitum. I could feel their comfort in the face of a loss that, even in the tiny shards I allowed myself to feel, I was unsure I would survive.

The skin across my entire body began to tighten and the walls seemed too close. I motioned to Lucy that it was time to leave and caught the pinball of glances from woman to woman across the table.

"What?" I asked.

They made a sacred offering: "We can tell you what she wanted at her funeral."

Of course they could. This group would have debriefed countless funeral Masses. They had a shared ethos of what made up the most holy tribute. Within a few minutes, I had my mother's entire Mass written out in the beautiful looping cursive that no one knows how to do anymore. As Lucy and I pushed our way out into the midday heat, we held on to the stern instruction not to be talked into hymn number fifty-six, which my mother had apparently said was "far too showy for a funeral."

TWENTY-THREE

The morning of my mother's service, I somehow got sand in my eye. My black dress, stockings, and makeup all set, my equilibrium was interrupted by one tiny grain. It hurt like hell.

I was patient at first. Standing at the bathroom vanity, I pulled my eyelid back and forth as one does, swishing with water. Within a minute I was stomping and screaming.

I slapped my toiletry kit from its perch on the sink, sending shimmering pinks and grays in their tiny jewel-shaped containers flying across the bathroom. The walls and floor were left looking like a nightclub covered in glitter rage. Something about the mess immediately soothed me.

Mike ran toward the noise, startling us both by flinging open the door, tie askew and panting. His face was laced with equal parts fear and confusion. He'd come on a rescue mission, but the heat of it blew straight through me.

"I could do without this!" I screamed. Mike's eyes widened like a little boy's.

I hadn't even noticed my tears had already dislodged the offending grain of sand.

In the movie version of my life, Mike and I hug. In reality, I mumbled, "Fuck this." Then I slipped past him in the door-frame, making sure our bodies didn't touch. I could not tolerate being comforted, physically or otherwise. Over the months when my father was dying, Mike had been gentle and tolerant of my anger, but it exhausted us both. I hoped this flare would pass but held myself tight as we drove the three miles to the funeral home in silence, just in case.

The parking lot at the church was still mostly empty when we arrived, though the service coordinator, Eva, was waiting for us. "Welcome," she said, and immediately shushed herself in embarrassment. I stepped into the church's inner foyer, where I winced in disgust at a *"Cape Cod Times* Finalist: Best Place to Worship" poster taped slightly askew to an interior door. I tugged down the page, crumpled it, and put it in Eva's stunned hands.

"No way," I said to her with emphasis. My mother's funeral was not open to a fucking Yelp review.

Not surprisingly, the LOLs were early arrivals. We pinned them like prom dates with blue-ribbon crosses we'd homemade with patience and a glue gun. Like a color-coordinated corsage at the homecoming dance, the pins would allow my mother's special team to be easily identified by everyone.

The beautiful photomontage that had become my sisters'

twenty-hour grief obsession was displayed at the entrance of the church. It showcased my mother's youth, beauty, and love of family. Her tiny frame, graceful glamour, and shy smile held its own against my father's big presence across fifty years of images. I stared for minutes trying to imagine her back to life.

My mother had been too overwhelmed to face other mourners at my father's funeral, so our family hid out in a small side chapel until the Mass began. This time my siblings and I, along with a smattering of our children, stood by the front doors of the church, greeting people as they entered. We found ourselves unexpectedly hugging loved ones we hadn't seen in years. My best and only friend from my farmhouse childhood, Jessica, came with her entire extended family. They had canceled a birthday party and taken planes, trains, and at least one ferry to get to us. "I'm so, so sorry," each member of her family said as my body went a golden sort of hazy at the sound of the long-ago familiar voices. For a moment I was sure I was ten again and my parents were still alive.

The organ vamped the beginning of the service, and I knelt in the pew next to my sister. I held Mike's hand. He kept his gaze forward, tears falling unchecked onto his lapel. He had loved and lost her too.

Somehow, during my streak of overfunctioning earlier in the week, I had insisted I should be the one to deliver my mother's eulogy. Catholics have very specific rules: you have exactly three minutes, mentioning only faith without exalting the dead. My brother's words at my father's funeral had been a master class, and he did not hide how difficult it had been. I'm not sure if I thought it was someone else's turn to shoulder the burden, if I thought my mom should be eulogized by a daughter, or if I wanted to be the center of attention; all were possible.

When the time came I stood and walked myself to the pulpit.

"Our mother gave to us, didn't she?" I read from the pages I had worked and reworked the day before. "She gave us the example of her love, the safety of her belief in us—each of us— and the security of her devotion. To many of us, particularly her children, she was and will remain the embodiment of home."

I managed not to cry, which is the one thing I am absolutely sure she would have truly wanted.

Hours after the reception, we held a family-only graveside service, where I found myself furious I'd forgotten to plan a hymn to sing. My mother had asked me to perform the traditional tune "How Can I Keep from Singing" at my father's service. Without her, her own hymn had been forgotten completely. I tucked my failure among the growing list. I did not consider how hard her death was for me, only how often I found myself failing in it.

Mercifully, as the sun sank over the perfectly clear day, our group of twenty-four mourner relatives found ourselves headed back to the beach. As if on cue, the five-o'clock light lit the beach house and cloaked the shoreline in a goldenrod easing into a warm amber.

I helped assemble an eclectic array of reception leftovers into a sort of dinner buffet on my mother's kitchen island as the others headed straight to the beach. I pulled a cookie from the pile I'd ridiculously overpurchased thanks to the live-event fifth-grade math problem I'd solved incorrectly during my catering order. (If you have 120 guests and each dessert plate has thirty-two cookies, how many trays should you buy? The answer, it turned out, was not five.) I slipped on flip-flops and headed toward the shrieks of laughter coming from the shore. From my parents' grassy hill, I could see my older brother running a complicated game of pickle with his grown son on the far base, my children and their cousins running in between.

The traces of the service shaken off with the shoes and suits up at the Big House, an observer from the parking lot might have envied a family lucky enough to enjoy a beautiful evening together. I begged off invites to join in the game and instead swung the leg of a mother, aunt, wife, and orphan over the sea wall, where I sat and watched.

The children ran as if on a playground. They high-fived, bumped bodies, and sprinted with a kind of joy that felt like a celebration of the normal and the alive. I felt a flicker of jealousy as my kids enjoyed their crowd of cousins with the meaning of the day seemingly forgotten. Like an outsider looking in, I was distracted by my awareness that this congregation was unlikely to gather again anytime soon.

I noticed a deep hollow of loneliness in my chest that gurgled almost like indigestion. For the first time in days, I had no to-do list. I wasn't already behind on anything. No one needed me in this moment but me. I sat, pressing a hand to my breastbone, wondering how I would know what to do next. I needed quiet and stillness and a minute to gather my thoughts, though I felt I could hardly trust them.

My youngest suddenly stopped running and motioned to the sky. He'd seen it first.

"Oh!" He pointed wordlessly to the expanse behind me, and I turned. An explosive chorus of oohs and aahs accompanied the burning electric-pink-and-orange sky. It looked as if someone had dipped enormous fingers in neon sunset colors and wiped them in one clear streak just above my parents' house.

"I've never seen a sky like it." The voice came from a group of runners literally stopped in their tracks by the ethereal light. I felt my chest fill with the sky's same warm, soft glow.

I whispered, "Okay, Mommy, we get it." It was the last time I would sense her presence for months.

Everyone made their way back up to the Big House, but I stayed on the seawall long after the sun bowed out to dusk. My arms and legs caught a chill as I watched the waves on the water and seagulls skittering at the ocean's edge.

This is not a problem. It's just different, I repeated to myself. I didn't notice when the words morphed to *I'm just different.* The sky continued to darken, and like the late arrival of an old friend, I watched Jupiter ease itself into its low-hanging early-evening spot, bright and familiar.

I thought of a story my father had told me when I was little about two sailors who got lost at sea during a hurricane.

"Did they live?" I asked him breathlessly.

"What do you think?" he replied. I was ten. I told him I was sure they had died.

"But they didn't die." My father's smile crept through as if he was about to reveal the trick behind the magic. "They waited until the clouds parted, pointed their instruments to the sky, and used a familiar star to guide them home."

Tumbling through the story for the first time as an adult, I realized I'd spent my entire life desperately trying to memorize the map of my night sky. I'd ignored the part about having reliable tools that might help me navigate when I needed them. I stared at the dark horizon as my head pulsed with an energy that felt exactly like the sensation of being lost.

TWENTY-FOUR

We were slated to leave my parents' house the morning after the funeral. I woke at 4:00 a.m. to steel gray cloud cover, which matched my mood. My siblings had announced plans that would seemingly return them back to their normal lives over the next few days. Mike had used up his time off, and our kids needed to get back to start school. I would leave my parents' lives and their deaths, but not because I was ready and not because I wanted to.

With dawn barely breaking, I walked across the damp lawn to the steps where my mother had spent her mornings for the better part of thirty years. When I was nearly to the patio, I came upon a large monarch butterfly lying still in the grass. I'd almost crushed it with my foot. Its wings covered in dew, the butterfly resembled a crumpled clump of colored tissue paper. I spoke to it directly. "Please don't be dead."

I bent down and scooped the insect into my hand, remembering a warning not to touch the wings of something... Was it birds or butterflies? Immediately, the creature's magnificent legs gripped my finger. Its wings made slow movements, but movements just the same. In and out. In and out. How many times had I heard my mother say "Meg! Come here! I need to show you something wonderful in nature!"?

I walked the border of my mother's garden with the butterfly still clinging to me. The sun rising in earnest, my bare feet chilled by the damp grass, I tried several times to gently shake the insect free.

"You don't need to die today," I cajoled.

I spied a large piece of driftwood sitting on a patio table in the glowing sun. Using my fingers and a hollow reed I'd pulled from the garden, I carefully transferred the grip of the butterfly's little legs.

Someone else surely would have thought it was a sign. I wasn't sure I even believed my mother would come back if she could. Would she help me do the impossible task of leaving, even if I was to blame for her death?

When my sister came outside a half hour later, I told her the story of the butterfly and pointed to where it had been. I wiped away two tears of relief when I saw that it was gone.

Soon the house and the yard filled with my siblings and their kids. A general plan formed. We would secure the house as if for the winter, disconnecting hoses, moving kayaks under the deck, taking in the garden statues and patio furniture. Inside the house, a few of us thought it best to move the obvious valuables—some china and crystal—away from the windows where they might invite the wrong kind of interest.

Everyone helped, and it was almost fun—like preparing for a party. Little ones carried bowls and lamps upstairs, bringing blankets and sheets back down. I tried to stay busy, keep in the flow, but I lost my breath on the landing and then again on the patio, where I threw the tangle of garden hose down in anger and defeat. Every movement scratched me like the remnant of a plastic tag left in the back of my shirt collar, just out of reach.

I couldn't stop the leaving, the drifting away. I could feel it in the wind, pushing and pulling. It was hard to discern which energy was a friend and which a foe. I stood in the swirl of the sea air, willing the atoms that were once my parents back to me.

Goodbyes came next, which felt anything but good. My brother needed to get kids back to colleges in faraway states; my sister and her family had a plane to catch; half of one brother's family had split after the funeral, and I somehow missed the farewell hugs. I found the ones offered now, especially from the littlest of my nieces, exquisitely painful. I had to touch my chest to check that my heart was still beating when the smallest little love waved from her booster seat as her car slipped down the slope of the driveway.

Mike, the kids, me, and my younger sister, who was around the back of the house watering our mother's garden for the final time, were all that remained. She was the only one who knew where to find the outside water spigots hidden under the house. We would ride together in our car as far as the

Providence train station, where my sister would then make her own way back to her New York City home.

I glanced at the heavy snowball heads of my mother's hydrangea, reliable year after year. At what point would they begin to die as well? Maybe my brother, the executor of the estate, would hire a gardener, a life-support system for the plants, until the house was inevitably sold and responsibility for life and death changed hands. The new homeowners would soon refer to the flowers as theirs, which would be correct but also not at all right.

I ran my hand along the honeysuckle lining the beach house driveway. Later, I would find its scent lingering on the oversized sweatshirt I'd found in my mother's closet and worn for successive days. Once back home, I did exactly what so many grieving clients had reported to me over the years—impulsively put out the unwashed sweatshirt on the curb for a charity pickup, only to change my mind an hour later and find it was already gone.

Standing at the door of the beach house, I realized too late I'd forgotten to bring the key. I held my hand to my forehead to cut the glare on the glass as I stared through the window of the tiny cottage—one of my top three favorite places on earth. I had locked myself out.

I turned and gazed across the gray water and wondered how much of my childhood and young adulthood I'd left scattered on this shoreline. I glanced toward the island and suddenly felt the need to sit down. As the past and present accordioned together, I slipped out of sight around the side of the house and

lay down in the forest-green deck chair that had already held
me for hundreds of hours of my life. I closed my eyes and put
my hands across my face.

I remained still even when I heard a car door open and shut
on the other side of the house and noted the weight of a person
striding across the deck toward me.

"You know I can see you, right?"

Maia. Of course she had come.

"I can't face this," I nearly whispered.

"Well, then, stay right like that. It might be a bit literal, but
I'm into it."

I felt her flop down heavily into the lounger next to me, and
my heart gave a small pulse of caring and exhaustion. These
had been impossible days for other people too.

I slowly spread my fingers out jazz-hands wide and peeked
through, finally dragging them down from my face and leaving
them to rest on my stomach.

"It's too much," I said, my voice cracking. "Like losing king,
queen, and country. I can't do it. I can't leave them."

Maia stayed quiet.

"It's not even my home..." My voice trailed off.

"But it's where they lived." She finished my sentence, and my
tears broke through. We'd always known the house would not
be shared by me and my siblings. My parents were clear about
their wishes. Even as devoted as we were to each other, it was
impractical for so many people to try and share one house.

"Where will they live in my mind if we don't have their
home?" As the words tumbled out, I understood my pain

better. When the house inevitably sold, my memories would be set loose. Where would I imagine my parents, think of them, or remember them?

Maia turned her face to mine.

"Maybe that's what you have to figure out."

We both felt the ground shudder slightly again. Like a fugitive surrounded, I knew my time truly was up. Mike and the kids had come to collect me. My choices dwindled; soon there would be no way out.

Maia and I both turned instinctively to the sound of more car doors opening and closing.

"Run down and say goodbye to the beach," I heard Mike call as three heads bounded down the trailhead's weather-beaten board, through the seagrass, and to the water.

"GOODBYE, BEACH!" The kids' voices were buoyant and silly, and almost immediately they were scrambling back up on the deck.

Maia popped up from her seat like an offensive lineman attempting to protect her quarterback. No kid made it through. I turned my head away from the hugs and "I love yous" they earnestly gave her, and she gave them back.

Hearing Maia and Mike's muffled voices, I realized by their easy tone they'd been talking around me and directly to each other for some days now.

"It's okay," Mike said gently to Maia. I wondered if either of them believed it. Were they talking about me? I was not okay. With every minute that ticked by, I could feel the adrenaline and disassociation that had buoyed me through the past week leaking from my body. Like a car losing oil, my gears were grinding to a halt, my engine destroyed. I neither wanted to nor believed I could really leave this place.

I listened to Mike herd the kids back into the car and clocked my sister's voice. The hour of our departure had truly arrived. In thick, heavy panic I pulled myself up from my lounge chair and caught my own scent. Rancid and rank, I felt repulsive. I was utterly unable to step into the hug Mike offered at the edge of the deck.

As I stood firm in the distance between us, I understood that I would not leave. I would go to the car where my sister and my children waited, pull out my backpack filled with darkness, dig out my newly cut keys looped on a teal bungee-style bracelet, and *stay*. I would just stay. I would open the beach house windows, turn on the ancient dial radio, and let the air and myself back in. I would not be angry when my family left me behind, and everyone would be grateful.

Maia stepped into the slow-motion silence between Mike and me.

"I brought something," she said. I dragged my eyes to focus and watched as she tapped at her phone.

"It's a poem. I'm going to read it." Her voice was quiet but firm.

My mind caught only snippets of "This Day We Say Grateful: A Sending Blessing" by Jan Richardson, but I would reread it so often later I would eventually learn it by heart.

On this day,
let us say
this is simply the way

love moves
in its ceaseless spiraling,
turning us toward
one another,
then sending us
into what waits for us
with arms open wide to us
in welcome
and in hope.

As the words drifted seaward, I felt my possibility pass. My mind could not catch up with the actions around me as Mike managed to finally pull me into the arms that I'd been avoiding. Maia's voice continued to ring like a priest's prayer over an execution.

O hear us
as this day
we say
grace;
this day
we say
grateful;
this day
we say
blessing;
this day
we release you
in God's keeping

in gladness
and love.

I lost the poem to the wind. Mike released me and wiped the tears that had blown across my cheeks with his sleeve. I hugged Maia, who put her hands on either side of my face and kissed my forehead. All words except one had left me: "Help," I whispered, and Maia waved Mike over. But it was too late.

I'd suddenly become so weak I needed Mike to ease me into the car. I leaned on his arm and used my hands to help pull my legs into the passenger side of the minivan. The bottom of my feet carried with them a fine, pinprick layer of sand.

"You okay?" Mike asked. There was no way to answer his question honestly, and I felt almost as if I had forgotten how to speak. I had no language for this. I gave him silence, which was all I had left.

The kids, the dog, my younger sister, and all my mother's house plants were positioned precariously in the back of the car. We drove a mile and a half to my sister's friend's house and parked outside while the two women found homes for my mother's beloved plants, many of which were older than my children. I felt convinced there was a notable change in oxygen as they closed the trunk of the car, now empty of the life my mother had tended.

The friend offered coffee in steel cups heavy with ice, and we took them with gratitude.

I felt my panic barely below the surface and sipped the cold coffee. I looked deep into the brown liquid brewed from the water that ran through the soil of this town, willing its hydro-gen and oxygen compound down into my cells, into the inter-nal spaces newly opened from the lack of her.

Mike drove south. We dropped off my sister at the train sta-tion, and when I slipped out of the car to hug her, I instantly understood I was at risk of not being able to get back in.

"I'll be fine," she assured me, but I clung to her like a bead from a necklace newly broken, slipping toward the floor. I would not be fine, and I could feel myself tumbling. I let her go because that was the way it had to be, but we both wiped our eyes as she walked away.

My youngest needed the bathroom, and Mike sent him walking toward me as I stepped heavily back toward the car.

"Mom?" Nick called out to me as I walked straight past him and almost did not turn at his voice. My mind floated, wonder-ing why my children even called me Mom. Was I really a mom? The word seemed suddenly absurd. Nicky slipped his hand in mine, and I couldn't tell who was leading whom. He asked to go to the men's room, a reasonable request at age seven, but I was accosted by the layers of city grime on the station floor, the smells of cigarette smoke, burned coffee, and stale donuts, and overly loud music from the window of a waiting taxicab.

The world felt truly unbearable as I pulled Nick into the ladies' room with force I barely had. He did not argue, and instead we both walked silently into separate stalls. Upon lock-ing the hollow metal door, repainted with hundreds of coats of shit-brown that the humidity left tacky to the touch, I swung around and vomited into the toilet. I saw Nicky's blue canvas sneakers freeze in the stall next door.

"You okay, Mommy?" There was that word again. What did it mean?

"Yep," I chirped, my voice as sickly cheerful as I could possibly make it.

I quickly sat down on the toilet and desperately gathered up the skirt of my T-shirt dress, stuffing it in my mouth to stifle the scream I could barely prevent. I flushed to cover the sound. I saw my little guy's feet standing at what must have been the sink, waiting for me. I imagined myself getting up, walking to the basin, and washing my hands and the two of us making our way out to the car together, but I felt no confidence I could make it happen.

Then suddenly we were back at the car, and somehow, I found my arm under Mike's shoulder again as he helped me jostle back into the front seat. He wiped more unnoticed tears from my cheeks with his thumb, the way one would an errant eyelash. He kissed my temple and ran back to the driver's side.

I cannot tell you how long we'd been driving. At some point I noticed my hand on the small metal latch of the car door. I do not know when my fingers found the handle, only that when they did, I couldn't pry them away. I knew for certain I would not open the door of a moving car but was terrified by the presence of an unfamiliar part of me that really hoped I might. Every muscle in my body clenched with the fear of discovering I had become my own threat to safety.

By the time we hit the inevitable Connecticut traffic, I'd lost track of the number of times I'd screamed at Mike to pull over. In slow and careful movements that filled me with rage, he would ease the car onto the road's shoulder so I could snap open my door and pop out like a jack-in-the-box. I understood I was scaring him. I understood I was scaring our children, but I also knew I could not stop.

I'd had panic attacks before but never like these. I physically felt each mile we drove away from my mother's house and the ashes of her life. I was consumed by the new pain of simply being in my body. My mind twisted with grief and offered the biblical phrase "rent asunder." I repeated it under my breath as you might a phone number you were afraid of forgetting. I felt my flesh unraveling, and when I looked down at my hands, I half expected to see bone. I could feel fear pulsing off my children and was suddenly overwhelmed by the need to save them from the tempest I'd become, lest I wreck our whole ship and everyone aboard.

"PULL OVER! OH MY GOD, PLEASE!" I screamed. I heard Mike whimper and one of our kids inhale a sharp breath as I slipped out of the car before it came to a full stop in a motel parking lot. I felt the grit of asphalt underneath me and inhaled the smell of exhaust and garbage that had been left out too long in the sun. I was infinitely better than I'd been inside the car.

Mike swept around to where my body had slipped down and curled itself up near the tire. I took in the anguish in his eyes and tried to explain to him that I wouldn't stop even if I could. This was what leaving felt like, and I was sure I would feel this way for the rest of my life. I begged him to leave me at the motel.

"You can't ask me to get back in the car. I can't. Please, baby, just leave me here." I crouched and sobbed. *Please.*

"But how will you get home?" Home. What did that word even mean? I spelled it in my head as I watched him watch me, but I could see him consider it. I could see him weigh the option of loving me best by abandoning me.

I tugged at the crack. "It's okay to just leave me. I'll check myself into this motel and then when I feel better..." Like an addict begging a doctor for pills, I couldn't see beyond the pain of this moment. Everything was a solid gray such that I couldn't distinguish my ocean of grief from the horizon. I would never be able to get myself home, and we both knew it. His face fell.

"God, I wish we had something to give you." His sentence waved like a white flag at the edge of the emotional battlefield where we'd both decided to surrender.

I clutched Mike's forearm with wide eyes and pulled myself up along the still open car door to where my phone lay on the seat. My clinician mind flickered like an Edison bulb. It was a Sunday, but I felt sure she would answer. *SOS*, I texted to the best psychiatrist I've ever known. As I watched the three dots pulsing her instant reply, I noticed she'd texted condolences a few days earlier that I had somehow missed.

Worst panic attacks of my life, I replied to her question mark.

Can you tolerate Benadryl? her words flickered back.

I couldn't believe we hadn't thought of it ourselves. Mike quickly found a pharmacy on Google Maps, shoved me into the front seat, and inched our car back into traffic.

Within an hour, I'd swallowed the pink pills and was fully stretched out in the back of the minivan with my kids piled in around me. Mike kept the window slightly cracked so the last remnants of sea air could stay in my lungs for as long as possible.

The eight-hour drive from my mother's house to ours took thirteen, though mercifully, I was sedated for the last five. When I got out of the minivan in our driveway, I never got back in. Believing the car to be my assailant, Mike took the minivan to a resale lot the following day and sold it for under blue book value to an overly friendly man named Kwon.

TWENTY-FIVE

We were home for only a day when the kids began their new school year. I wasn't anywhere near ready to go back to work. I texted my clients that I would be out for another two weeks. Lack of sleep had become a problem. It wasn't uncommon for me to be awake from 3:00 to 6:00 a.m., then go back to bed for an hour or two just as the kids were getting up. My functioning hours were hardly predictable.

The invitations to return to "regular life" came as soon as we flipped on our porch light. It was the signal that we had made it back from our extended month of summer-bereavement vacation, if not altogether safely.

Friends called and texted, suggesting we go for lunch or meet up at a park or on my porch. "Sounds great," I would reply, already knowing I would cancel a few hours beforehand.

I knew what I was doing. I couldn't eat, and in my experience starving yourself, inadvertently or not, is something other women tend to notice. I found it impossible to be around people who knew the helpful, friendly, confident, and clearheaded version of me when I no longer felt like her.

When we got the notice of my son's upcoming back-to-school night, I knew immediately it was a bad idea for me to go. As a mom of three with dozens of school events under my belt, I'd come to understand back-to-school night as more an opportunity for parents to size each other up rather than to learn about curriculum content.

Mike was on a business trip in Norway. There had been talk of me going with him, but I don't think anyone thought I was in any shape to get on a plane (and, oddly, there was little talk of him staying behind). Mike called from time zones away just an hour before the event was set to start. I casually announced my plan to skip it.

"I just can't bring myself to give a shit," I explained wearily. Mike understood, but my nine-year-old who appeared out of nowhere Bambi-ed his eyes slightly, betraying the fact he'd been eavesdropping. I clocked his flicker of fear, and after I hung up, I knelt down to his eye level and asked, "Did you hear me tell Daddy that I'm not going to do your classroom visit?"

He nodded silently. His mouth turned down in a hard frown.

"Just tell me if it's important to you, kiddo." I was leading the witness.

His mouth popped open like a sock puppet's, and the sentence fell apart on his tongue.

It's hard to raise emotionally honest *and* compliant children.

I nodded, waiting for him to continue, showing off my best therapist-parenting move of outwaiting silence.

"Well, I wrote you a note. It's on my desk." I felt an internal tug as I imagined my little guy composing a letter to me in his careful handwriting.

After missing an entire month of third grade with a protracted sinus infection yet still earning straight As, my son had argued his way into the faster-paced program for fourth grade. He was competitive, school mattered to him, and my refusal to play my part was creating anxiety he didn't deserve.

"And it's just... It's a new... Well, we don't know anyone." He sounded like he might cry.

I admired his use of the collective noun "we" and felt my resolve crumble. The boundary of his needs and my needs mixed together in the emotional rubble.

I sighed audibly.

"Okay, kid. You're right. I'll do it."

He threw himself around my waist in a rare display of emotional enthusiasm, and I thought, *This is where I am—my child is desperately relieved at my ability to parent at a basic level.* Like an old siren song, shame called to me from a distance.

"Thanks, Mommy." When I soothed fears or granted wishes, I was always Mommy, not Mom.

I made a game show–style phone-a-friend call to discuss what I should wear. It wasn't just that I'd lost the ability to remember which labels made up the parental school uniform, I'd also lost all my give-a-fucks.

"I haven't worn a bra or any shoes but flip-flops in about three weeks," I told Maia.

"Well, underwear is a must. I'd also suggest some sort of wrap dress and maybe a ballet flat or something. You have those, right?"

I replied that I did, but I no longer had a body that was comfortable wearing them. "It's only an hour," Maia said, coaching me. "You can do anything for an hour."

I wasn't confident she was right, but after the sitter arrived, I drove the easily walkable distance to the school and got myself inside by employing a technique I've suggested to hundreds of clients anxious about entering social gatherings: come in late and on the phone.

Once I got through the door, I popped my cell to my ear and immediately noticed my ragged breathing. I nodded hellos to familiar faces in the hallway, sports parents I knew from Saturday sidelines, and friendly classroom moms. It was the largest number of people I'd seen since my mother died. Everyone was oh-so-likable and the same. I found them all terrifying.

I swept into the classroom five minutes past the start time, still on my imaginary call about something "I won't be able to handle until I am out of this meeting." My hair was at least combed, if not clean. I felt sure I passed as a normal, functioning parent in my swishy dress and simple shoes with heavy gold medallions on the toe. I avoided the close-up inspection of the mothers. Emotionally alert female small talk felt too threatening. I found my son's desk, where I sat and read his note, gratefully ignored by the two dads adjacent to me who were engrossed in a conversation about under-ten lacrosse.

"Welcome, parents! I am Ms. Dee, and I am so thrilled and

honored to be teaching your fourth-graders this year!" Goodness, she was perky.

"I'm really looking forward to getting to know your children. I have already had a chance to have quick one-on-one chats with each of my students. I am confident this is going to be a very special year." She paused for breath and a parent somewhere toward the front of the room made things more ridiculous by clapping.

Ms. Dee continued. "This is my third-year teaching. I also teach fitness classes on the weekends, and I love camping. In fact, I just checked off another item on my bucket list: camping in Alaska with my mom for a month for her seventy-seventh birthday."

Suddenly I was lit up from the inside, engulfed by wild flames of uncontrollable hatred for the teacher. I imagined the walls of the classroom melting from the heat radiating from me. I found myself quickly rapt in the brutal math of loss. How could she have gotten more years and days and minutes with her mother than me? The injustice tasted sour, like a day's worth of hunger.

I missed everything Ms. Dee said for the next several minutes as the part of me that was still a therapist tried deep breathing to regulate myself. I pinched my palms with my fingernails in the hopes of pulling myself out of the past and back into the present. My mind recalled the acronym I often taught my clients: STUG—subsequent temporary upsurge of grief. Coined by the clinical psychologist and loss researcher Therese Rando, STUG is a grief term I've always liked that reminds us that grief comes out of nowhere, obliterates, then passes.

At long last, the lights went down, and a presentation started.

I noticed bodies beginning to stir in the slightly darkened room, like when the lights are still dimmed and the credits roll at the movies. The overheads flicked on, and I heard a voice from the parent group. I realized Ms. Dee was taking questions.

The mother's voice was clear.

"I understand that there was a conversation about death during morning meeting yesterday?" Her voice turned up on the last word—a vocal mannerism favored by a younger generation.

It was the angle of Ms. Dee's head nod that made me realize I was standing.

"I'm just wondering if we think that kind of conversation is really appropriate for kids this age?"

Ms. Dee's eyes locked with mine, both of us held hostage.

"Well . . ." The teacher's cheeks reddened. I realized she was really very young.

The mother continued with her back to me while other parents shifted uncomfortably.

"I mean, my son was really upset. I've heard great things about the counselor here. Will a referral be made?" The mother paused, clearly waiting for an answer, and when she didn't get one, she continued, "I'm just *so concerned* for that poor child."

Hurricane winds rushed inside my head, and ice ran down my arms. My torso morphed into an empty crystal bowl: brittle, precious, and precarious.

The teacher made no sudden moves but instead replied

slowly, while maintaining eye contact with me, "Yes, during morning meeting yesterday, when the children were asked about their summers, a student did share about a death."

I felt myself crumple at her words. I imagined my tiny, sweet, heartbroken boy, sitting in circle time, crisscross applesauce, telling his truth to a group of distracted, asshole kids. I bent at the waist, holding myself upright against the grief, hands on my thighs like a runner gasping for air. One of the fathers behind me gently placed a wide palm on my back. Startled, I instinctively snapped upright.

"You are referring to *my* son."

My voice was shaky with anger but clear. I choked to regain control of my sob and exhaled myself back to courage. My fury and sorrow filled the whole room, and every particle of oxygen was consumed by it. I widened my legs to steady my stance.

"Thank you so much for your *concern*; my children talk about their feelings and tell the truth when asked, but I'll make sure my son knows not to do that in *this* classroom again." I cleared my throat in triumph and, as if flashing my credentials, added, "I'm a trauma therapist."

Only, of course, I didn't actually say or do any of those things.

Instead, my body resorted to a plain old panic attack. I lost my ability to speak, my breath went shallow, and I nearly fainted. The man who'd previously tried to help generously guided me out of the room. The entire exchange likely lasted a whole of three minutes.

In the life that had broken away from me, I had been a verb. "Meghan-ing (v): to destroy a person emotionally with the verbal acuity honed as a middle child of five siblings." My traumatized mind moved too slow, and grief had all but extinguished my access to anger, particularly the righteous kind. I had been missing for more than a month, my own face on a milk carton.

I don't remember how I got home, but I do remember sitting bolt upright in bed at 3:00 a.m. as I had the night before and would again in the nights to come, my mind echoing with the same relentless thought: *It's my fault she died.*

When I woke again at 5:00 a.m., I was coming out of a dream so vivid I wrote it down in its entirety: I'm in the kitchen of my mother's house, standing at the sink. I'm staring out toward her back garden of white Casa Blanca lilies. There are more than usual. I'm washing a soapy glass bowl, which is unwieldy, and I'm trying not to drop it. My back is to the room.

Suddenly my mother is at my shoulder, all five feet of her. I look down, ready to say something insignificant and sarcastic, when she looks up at me with a sheepish smile of apology. Her eyes widen, and in the same moment, we both realize that she died.

And I drop the bowl.

Instantly, I scoop her into an urgent, fierce hug. My hands drip soap on her tiny birdlike frame. She whispers something I can't hear with my ear crushed to her shoulder in the hug we know by heart. It might be "I'm sorry."

And, as if knowing I could never let her go, in my dream she lets go of me instead.

TWENTY-SIX

After my father died, I lost the concentration required to read books. My mind would cloud over and lose any train of thought. Three weeks after my mother died, I couldn't stop reading. Each day, Amazon dropped another bleak-titled tome on our doorstep that Mike would bring in for me to tear open and read until I threw it across the room.

I searched for myself in others' words, though I knew no person could truly capture the precarious web of thoughts and feelings weaving across my heart in those early weeks. I slept through the day, read at night, and mostly opted out of everything.

The CNN-like ticker of traumatic images of my mother's and sometimes father's dead bodies was relentless. To cope, I leaned into the self-care I typically recommended to my clients. Exercise helps create endorphins and regulate sleep and hunger. I decided swimming might be less punishing than my usual run. I craved the sun and the solitude, and our outdoor community pool was virtually empty during the newly odd hours I found myself awake.

I slipped on an old maternity tankini that was loose-fitting and generously easy to get on and off and brought a small bag of items: no dive sticks or inflatables but instead a large thermos of contraband iced coffee and a few crackers for a post-swim snack. If my laps, two freestyle, one breaststroke, were excruciatingly slow, only the teenage guard was there to notice. I enjoyed this gentle routine for nearly a week.

On the fourth day, I left the pool with water trapped in my ear. More annoying than painful, I tried all the tricks. I kicked out my opposite leg while shaking my blocked ear vigorously. Jumped up and down. Nothing.

For two days, I used over-the-counter earwax treatments before finally walking into a nearby urgent care, where I was immediately redirected to an ENT clinic. The doctor who greeted me explained his specialty was rhinoplasty—he was just subbing in for someone who was out sick. He employed a dizzying water-blasting technique, took one look inside my ears, and said the words no patient ever wants to hear: "Cool! I've never seen *this* before."

With the glee of a teen gore enthusiast, he explained I had developed a condition called exostosis, or "surfer's ear," caused by prolonged exposure to cold water or wind. Small bones had grown across the interior of my ear canal, eventually causing the blockage. The growths would impact my hearing completely if left untreated.

The doctor claimed that a life raised on a beach was to blame, but twenty years as a therapist had taught me that we grieve with our bodies. Loss has the power to transform us physically in unimaginable ways. I almost liked the idea that my ears had grown gates, threatening to close my mind off from any other terrible thing the world might want to tell me.

The doctor rattled off information I was unable to retain. I understood the problem to require surgery (it did) immediately (it did not). I'd come in looking for help but now had so much water sloshing around in my head that I was too disoriented to drive. Mike was still on his work trip, so I took an Uber home.

From the back of the car, I called the surgeon's office, but it went straight to voice mail. I left a rambling message, omitting my callback number, and then quickly consulted my most trusted medical expert, Google.

The thing about searching for answers to ease anxiety is that your brain is in such a state of alert, it skews the information to seem more threatening. It was no surprise that the sages of the internet sent me into full-fledged panic. I found little information about the surgery, though nearly every entry described the ear being cut off the head and the bones removed with a drill. Several reports included how many days "out of the water" each surfer suffered, but there was little information on what to expect for an out-of-shape forty-five-year-old mother's recovery.

By the time the car deposited me home, I was in full despair. I walked past my kids and their sitter engrossed in a game of cards while I hurried upstairs for a few moments of privacy. Closing the bedroom, bathroom, and shower doors, I slid down on the tiled floor and screamed into a towel.

I felt a hollow ache in my chest where I used to feel my mother. I yearned to hear her imperfect attempts at support, even though my siblings and I always laughed that she was not super-tolerant of physical frailty. When I was injured in high school (herniated disc) or sick in college (walking pneumonia), she'd heavily implied I had caused my own health issues. At that moment, I craved her dismissal. It was better than her acute absence. I struggled to wrap my head around the fact that I'd be having surgery without her silent worry or prayers.

I sat on the cold bathroom tile and cried about my broken heart and body. From my vantage point on the floor, I took a picture of my legs and feet curled on the bath mat, a subtle reference to all the stories where the heroine ends up in a middle chapter on the bathroom floor. When I checked my phone days later, I could see the nuance of the photo did not translate well.

I texted a few friends, including Maia, saying something like *Bad things getting worse*, explaining what I thought was true—I would have to organize an emergency surgery in the next day or so. Maia called immediately. I remember I was sobbing.

Where was Mike? she demanded. Could I call friends to come help? I explained that one close friend was in an all-day meeting. Another had just gone out of town. Maia ticked through the names of other people in my entourage while I responded with reasons why none were available. Maia knew me well enough to know I didn't want company, but at her distance it was hard to know whether my decision was just stubborn or dangerous.

Eventually, Lucy knocked on the bathroom door in tears about something. A classmate? A teacher? I abruptly hung up with Maia and left my phone on the bath mat with the ringer off as usual.

Lucy insisted her misery would be best solved by takeout and a movie. The three kids and I snuggled in a pile on the big couch in the basement and watched *High School Musical*. I explained my puffy eyes by saying, "I am just having a hard, sad day."

"Are you crying, Mommy?" my littlest asked.

"I was crying. I'm okay now." I sighed deeply.

"Because of Nana?" He snuggled in closer.

"Because of Nana but also because something is wrong with my ears and the doctor made me feel scared and helpless."

Scary doctors were something we all understood. I drifted into an hour-long light sleep with the kids scrunched up in various positions against me and Zac Efron crooning in the background.

The sound of the doorbell was disorienting. Both my middle son and I stumbled upstairs to see a neighbor standing shyly on my front porch. I opened the door to accept the carafe of iced tea she held. It felt like an odd offering, and I could tell something was off.

I heard "worried" and "safety" and an invitation to sleep at her house. I can't remember if I was gracious. I just started talking.

"It's been a long day, Jackie," I replied heavily. "I have to have surgery, and I'm a little freaked and super-tired."

"Yes, I heard." Jackie stood smiling as my mind tried to calculate how that was possible. Jackie was a neighbor but not a friend who I would have expected to "hear" anything.

"Well, I offered to come over. People were worried." She said it like she'd been elected head of an invisible committee.

"Well, thanks again," I said, though I did not really mean it and somehow managed to thank her out the door.

I went in search of my phone.

There were many texts from Maia and a few other friends as well. There was also one voice mail from Mike. He was on his way to the airport. He'd be home as soon as he could.

I believe my exact words were "What the actual fuck?"

I scrolled quickly through the messages without fully reading, gleaning the general gist.

My call had scared Maia, and when I didn't answer her later calls and texts, she went from scared to terrified.

I wanted to feel bad for scaring Maia, but I didn't. I texted her and told her I was fine and going to bed. Possibly alert to my increasing frailty, all three kids asked to sleep in my room.

At zero dark thirty, I woke as usual, my mind offering me the previous day's situation with clarity. Maia had been afraid I was going to kill myself with my three kids in the house.

I peeled myself away from my slumbering children and out of my bed in a wild fury. Even my longest and most perfect best friend since age eleven had completely misunderstood me. I was nowhere near contemplating suicide, and her belief that

I was felt like an accusation of child abuse and neglect. In my righteous rage, I stomped around my kitchen, having an imaginary conversation: "I *know* my limits. I would *never* put my children at that kind of risk. What kind of a *person* could think that of *me*?" It took hours for the anger to melt out of my hurt. Even though I truly, deeply believed suicidality was an illness where no one was at fault, some part of me must have also believed it was controllable because I took Maia's suggestion as an insult, not a signal of care.

A previous version of me would have been angry at myself for scaring Maia, but this one was just angry at her. We hadn't practiced much anger between us, and the timing made it impossible to learn now.

I texted Maia: *It's either okay for me to be as I am or it isn't. Check in with Mike from now on.* I did not try to hide. I resented the idea that I should have to worry about her feelings. In trauma work we talk about a "window of tolerance"—a Goldilocks-style bandwidth of optimal experience of not-too-much and not-too-little emotion. My window was becoming smaller and smaller, and Maia had just exploded the panes into fine glass dust. I didn't talk to her again for a month.

What pain obscured completely, of course, was the important signal that I had managed to terrify my best friend. She was the woman who knew me better than nearly anyone and had already seen me through my darkest times. Maia had been wrong about the *self*-harm but not the harm. My mother's death was making me sick, and unsurprisingly, my lifelong best friend was the first one to see it.

TWENTY-SEVEN

My insistence that I attend the standing Monday lunch with my supervision team a month after my mother's death was a last-ditch effort to hold on to my beloved old life. Our group of single practitioners had been created more than a decade ago to support each other through client work and motherhood. We met at someone's house with questions about cases and with babies in tow. Now, with kids in school, we had graduated to a high-end farm-to-table restaurant, where we ordered kale salads, discussed treatment recommendations, and wept occasionally needed tears into the pressed linen napkins.

I stepped into the nearly empty restaurant in clothes that felt too tight and limbs that felt too loose and made my way to the table where Maribeth and Stacy were already seated. Between us, we had fifteen years of friendship and case collaboration. I was grateful to see them.

Could they tell I had to have my husband button my sweater? I was sure I looked as out of place as I felt, though I wouldn't have dared to check that fact in a mirror. Shell shock radiating off me, I waved to my friends, who greeted me with awkward phrases of "You look good" and "I'm so sorry."

"Thank you for coming," I said as they hugged me. It was the same phrase I'd used at the funeral, the only words I could rely on. Sometimes I believed my mother's death was just the beginning of everything worse instead of the ending of everything good.

There was a millisecond of conversational dead air, and my mind flashed the picture of my dead mother's hand gently curled, still clad with rings, fingertips blue, as if bruised. I shook my head to clear it, knowing the image would likely circle back into the forefront of my mind in a minute or so. I said nothing to Maribeth and Stacy. Instead, I watched the ice cubes shifting in a glass of water and felt the texture of the menu between my fingers. Everything appeared normal but felt different. The world went comfortably on even though my mother was no longer a part of it. I wasn't sure I was either.

Maribeth turned to me. "How are you, really?" Her kind dark eyes gazed into mine.

I turned my tears away. I didn't want to withhold the truth; I just didn't want to have to face it myself.

"I don't know who to be anymore," I said, testing the only words that made sense.

Maribeth pressed my hand, and both our eyes filled. "I know who you are," she said gently. I appreciated her effort, but she had never met this version of me before.

I had come to lunch with an ask. Though edges of me had eroded, the therapist in me knew to ask for this piece of help.

"How long do you think I should take off?" I braced myself for their answers.

"Six months." Stacy's voice was strong, unapologetic. These women knew trauma, and they knew me. The number was six times what I'd expected. I was equal amounts surprised and relieved. Allowing myself this much time was a stunning privilege, especially since most employers offer three days of bereavement leave. But we all agreed that me going back to work anytime soon was impossible.

TWENTY-EIGHT

The human body is brilliant and exquisitely wired toward safety and healing. In both my work and personal experience, I've learned that if you ignore the cues, the body will find its own way to get your attention. The back spasm the day after my supervision lunch should have been predictable.

Swimming had been declared a no go until after my ear surgery, which was scheduled in a month and a half. Clinging to the hope I might still claw myself back to mental and physical stability, using all the treatment and self-care practices I'd spent years suggesting to clients, I opted for an on-demand yin yoga video in my basement. Thought to move trapped emotions through the body, yin is popular in the trauma community. I'd taken many classes with an instructor friend who had since moved across the county. She taught me that yin offers stretches that are held for minutes at a time to allow for tension release that moves past muscles and instead goes deep into the fascia, where pain and trauma is believed to be held.

I'd only just made it downstairs to the basement and rolled out my mat when a violent back spasm threw me to my knees. The impact was so strong, it left my shins bruised for the next month. Akin to labor, my back pain intensified, then lessened but wouldn't release. I called upstairs.

"ANYONE! CAN ANYONE HELP?" Even yelling hurt. I heard small feet thudding quickly, and my nine-year-old son came down.

With his brave face flushed with fear, he encouraged me to try and lean my weight on his slight frame.

"I'm strong, Mommy. I can hold you."

I couldn't rouse myself from the floor. We were both in tears after I accidentally snapped, "Forget it. Just go get Daddy." I hated myself and my anger.

As my son went searching for Mike, our team's other grown-up, I tried to slip into a quick child's pose, hoping to stretch and release the muscles. No go.

My husband took one look at me on the floor and went running back upstairs in search of leftover painkillers and muscle relaxers from my last back spasm.

Over the years, I have learned that sharp twinges in my lower back are physical smoke signals saying "Slow down, pay attention, do less." The spasm after my father's death had been exceptionally bad. At one point, paralyzed and in pain, I begged my husband to call the paramedics. Once at the ER, I was intrigued to learn that along with painkillers, I'd been given Ativan—an antianxiety medication prescribed to several of my clients to manage panic attacks. The doctors had clearly seen my kind of mind-body corruption before.

Mike bore the brunt of my incapacity over the next two days. As I was unable to crawl to the bathroom, roll over, or support my weight in any meaningful way, he was forced to create a sort of bedpan situation. I didn't even have the energy to feel humiliated.

At some point I realized my abject vulnerability was likely what my mother had been talking about when she unintentionally hurt my feelings on our wedding day. I wasn't yet in my white dress with the gorgeous pearl detail when she said, "You think today is the most important day of your life with Mike, but that's because you can't imagine how you will be called upon to care for each other in the future."

The pain of how right she'd been, and how absent she was, made me weep.

Our basement was cave-like, with little natural light. It did nothing to improve my mood. I tried to lie still and ate and drank very little given what the bathroom situation required. Mike kept me on a consistent painkiller schedule, which meant I was lucid for only one hour out of every three. In the intervening hours, my mind found itself spinning in the memories of my mother's dead body while repeating the phrase "It's your fault" over and over again.

I had been trying to track the frequency of the images over the past week. I knew they had long since crossed the line from grief that resolved on its own into something else. My symptoms were getting worse and not better. I knew this relentless blame cycle was clinically an overreaction. I also knew I would be unlikely to get myself out of it.

I had a vague sense that my current destruction was born of some aspect of my untreated childhood trauma, and, during those rare moments of clarity, I wondered if my mother's death had triggered the reaction of something akin to a not-quite-healed infection. Buried emotions were erupting, clawing their way to the surface, and I wasn't sure I had the courage to face them. I knew what would have to come next.

I was writhing in breakthrough pain, waiting out the minutes before a new round of pills, when the doorbell rang. I heard the voice of my daughter's best friend.

"Do you want to come over?" she asked cheerfully.

There was a long pause before Lucy replied, "I think I should stay and help my mom. She might need me."

The children had mostly kept away from me for those few days while I marinated in my failure at everything. I had been running a story that my emotions were hardly impacting them. Lucy's words shattered the pretense.

Was I even really a mother anymore? I wouldn't be back to work for at least six months. Was I still a therapist? I'd stopped returning calls from siblings and friends. Could I still call myself a sister or a friend? It felt like only a matter of time before Mike would also realize I wasn't much of a wife. Everywhere my thoughts turned, they bounced off a fun house mirror's distorted reflection. I suddenly looked and felt as I had when I was a child—afraid and alone. How I felt was becoming who I was.

• • •

On my third basement morning, Mike brought down the food I'd need to eat before taking the last pain pills he'd somehow managed to scrounge up. I refused both. With tears of desperation and a rarely raised voice, Mike begged me.

"*Please* just let me take care of you."

Rigid with pain, grief, and mounting fear, I screamed at him, "You CAN'T take care of me! Lucy can't take care of me! *I* can't take care of myself! We can't do this on our own! WE NEED MORE HELP! *I need more help.*" Terror dressed as rage, and my whole body shook in the raw truth of myself.

I thought of my proud father asking me for help before he died. I suddenly realized what that must have required of him. I was no one's prisoner except my own. It was my own body and mind that had betrayed me.

I sobbed. Mike wept, and my pain level increased to intolerable. I eventually fell asleep while Mike gently rubbed his hand across my forehead and hair.

When I woke alone hours later, I realized *this* was what Maia had meant. Stacy and Maribeth too. In their own way, they had all suggested that I ask for more help. Killing yourself is not the only way to lose a life. Mine was slipping away before our eyes.

I called my friend and colleague Susan, who is brilliant and no-bullshit. An exceptional therapist and extraordinary friend, she had been checking in daily. In previous weeks, I'd made light references to wanting to "get away," which she alternately challenged or ignored. Susan had lost her mother a few months after my dad died. She knew grief, she knew trauma, and she knew I'd make this call.

I wiped my tears on the sleeve of my sweatshirt. "I need help," I said with a sniff.

"Next level of care?" she asked. Like a visit from an old friend, part of me perked up at the therapy lingo for inpatient hospitalization. We both knew that the need for hospitalization wasn't just about suicidality. Intensity of symptoms required intensity of care. I most often recommended inpatient care when a client's symptoms didn't abate despite the once- or twice-weekly sessions in my office.

I'm not sure I took Susan the least bit seriously when she said it, but I'd been in the game long enough to know my compass was pointing in only one direction. I was unable to get myself to my own therapist's office, and our sporadic phone check-ins would never be enough.

"Give me a few hours, I'll make some calls," Susan said. "I've got you." She hung up, but I kept the receiver to my ear, unsure what I'd just agreed to. Surely I was making too big a deal of this. I called myself a giant baby, which was actually accurate, since all I really wanted was my mom and dad.

When Susan called back an hour later, she'd already consulted several trusted colleagues. I wasn't surprised to hear they'd all suggested the same well-respected trauma center in Tennessee called Foundations. Each of us had sent clients there. Susan and I both knew the program cost tens of thousands of dollars and that stays could extend past the suggested four initial weeks. I felt myself floating slightly as my mind insisted the cost and the length of time away from my kids were impossible.

I felt terrible for wasting Susan's time, but more than that, I feared disappointing her.

"It's too expensive, too long." My voice cracked in shame.

I knew what Susan would say next. For a moment I hovered between therapist and patient.

"It *is* expensive, it *is* a long time, but you need to get well. You have C-PTSD, and it needs treatment, which I know you know."

It was clarifying to hear the letters said out loud. Complex post-traumatic stress disorder. I knew my diagnosis was so significant I would never be able to treat it by myself. The addition of the word "complex" signaled that it was, in fact, connected to childhood. This wasn't the grief that researchers assure us will resolve day by day over time. My mother's death had swept away everything in my life that was stable, leaving behind old and new pain. As experienced as I was, it was too much for me to address alone.

I heard the echo of Lucy's voice saying she needed to stay home to help me instead of going to play with her friend. I saw the pain in Stacy's and Maribeth's faces as they sat with me at lunch. I heard Maia's panicked voice and saw the increased frequency with which my siblings had been checking in on me. I thought of Mike and the way he gripped me while I sobbed and raged, neither of us able to help the other. I looked at my phone. I looked around the basement, where I had been living for the past three days.

I let go.

I stopped clutching any belief of finding my "before," and I yielded to trauma and the truth.

Okay, I texted Susan. *I'll go.* She immediately replied with a thumbs-up emoji.

When he came downstairs later, I shook as I told Mike the plan, terrified he would tell me it wasn't possible.

"We'll use our anniversary money," he replied. I could feel he was relieved to have something practical to offer. Our long-saved pennies intended for a week in Mexico to celebrate our fifteen years of marriage were traded for my three-week trauma treatment stay.

Once the plan was settled, I fell into an hour of deep, peaceful sleep. When I woke, my back unlocked completely. I walked upstairs for the first time in three days and kissed my kids' heads as they cheerfully and quietly played a board game.

It would be a year before I learned that Mike had borrowed the rest of the money from my oldest brother to afford my treatment. I wept in gratitude for both of them when I found out.

TWENTY-NINE

I woke up my first morning at Foundations disoriented and afraid. My mind offered me a grace period of twenty seconds before it reminded me my mother had died. A week ago, it had been ninety seconds, but just as the trauma books promised, my brain was beginning to update with new data. Soon, my memory would absorb the liminal space left from my before life, offering me only the devastation of after. In just a few days' time, my mind would no longer have to search to remember her death. It would become memorized like a vocabulary word of a language I would one day become fluent in.

I showered, feeling better rested than I had been in weeks. A notoriously light sleeper, I was surprised to find my roommate Rachel had managed to slip out without waking me. I sat on the bed, towel-drying my hair and hoping I might have the strength and coordination to dress myself.

· · ·

At check-in I'd been given an agenda with specific times and places to be, but I remembered little from my brief tour of the facility the previous day. I followed the sounds of voices and the smell of sausage, feeling confused and self-conscious. I found my way to the small cafeteria, where, like a high school freshman, I stood paralyzed, wondering if I should get food or try to find a place to sit. If I'd expected a somber, depressed atmosphere of illness, this was not it. The dining room was abuzz with people moving with purpose and tables full of crackling conversation. Mercifully, I found another human at my elbow.

"You new?" His voice was deep, his smile gleaming. I nodded. "Come on. Come sit with the cool kids." He chuckled and handed me a tray.

I teared up at his kindness and followed him through the buffet line, accepting large spoonfuls of food that were portioned onto my plate. I wondered whether he was staff or a client. At the table I met four other clients and learned my new friend was a client named Ian. From what I could see in the dining hall, our ages—twenties to midsixties—seemed like the biggest variable between us. There were equal numbers of men and women, and everyone was white and, given the price tag, I assumed wealthy.

I was startled by the number of times someone asked, "What brings you to treatment?" The question was invasive and way too intimate to be asked by a stranger. Also, I couldn't answer it. Barely choking out the words "My mother died" seemed insufficient, even if it was true.

After breakfast we were supposed to meet around the large fireplace for an update on the day's comings and goings from Andrea, the clinical coordinator. I seemed to be early. They'd taken my phone; I didn't wear a watch, and my natural body rhythm was off from the lack of sleep. I tucked myself into the corner of the couch and glanced at the clock on the fireplace mantel. If I'd been at home, my kids would have been walking out the door for school. I felt relief where maybe guilt should have been.

My weekly schedule indicated that group therapy met each morning in a small cabin near the Med Shed. I spent my first session watching a client work through an issue with her mother in a role play. I introduced myself to the four-member group but otherwise didn't say a word.

Lunch was promptly at noon.

"Oh, you'll love Dr. G.," my lunch table reported unanimously. I was still too exhausted to feel any kind of way about the doctor or much of anything else, but I appreciated the encouragement. Near the top of the hour my tablemates began to peel off to next activities.

After the lunch I couldn't eat; I still had a few extra minutes. Called by the huge leather couch sitting just outside the dining hall, I flopped down and reflexivity stuffed my hand down the arm as I did at home, rescuing all manner of things—forks, TV clickers, and the occasional half-eaten apple left by careless kid hands. This time I found the *New York Times* crossword puzzle with eleven down and twenty-six across already filled in. There had been a time when I'd done the crossword puzzle daily. I stared at the grid, missing the brain that had once loved to crack codes.

Suddenly, Dr. Grover swept in through the swinging doors.

"There you are," he said warmly. I'd completely forgotten our meeting.

"It's so unlike me to forget," I said, starting to apologize.

"Don't even worry about it."

Tall and in his midfifties, the doctor had kind eyes and a wide smile surrounded by a neatly trimmed beard. "Dr. G.," he said as he extended his hand. I shook it, unsure whether he planned to sit or if I should stand.

"Want to walk and talk? It's a beautiful day." Dr. G. gestured to the French doors that led toward the vast lawn.

My soupy memory surfaced a recollection of taking jittery teenage clients on walks. Movement shifted the intensity of trauma while allowing the brain to rewire some experiences. I nodded and wondered if having a chaperone for my first real trip outside was part of my treatment plan.

"So, two deaths two years apart is a lot on a person." Dr. G. looked at me as he spoke. "I bet your body was just barely getting back to normal from your dad's death when your mom died." I nodded. He spoke comfortably and confidently, explaining I had been hit by an "emotional tornado of sudden loss."

I toggled between wanting Dr. G. to take care of me and to be impressed by me. Ultimately, when my brain failed to form cohesive, impressive therapist thoughts, I landed on the former.

"The amygdala is the brain's smoke alarm." He smiled easily as he quoted Bessel van der Kolk. Dr. G. pointed to the back of his skull, just as I always did, to the place where the head and neck meet. "Trauma causes the amygdala to enlarge and choke off signals that would normally travel up and across the rest of the brain. The blockage impacts mood, sleep, hunger, concentration, memory, and even decision-making." I nodded. I knew this description by heart. "When we describe someone as traumatized, we mean the brain is ringing like a gong from a hard piece of information it took in. It may be months, even years, before the brain can even itself out again. The amygdala means well, but it can really screw you over."

I smiled for the first time in an eternity. Dr. G.'s straightforward ease reminded me of my old self.

"Our techniques are everything you would expect and some things you might not," he said before describing the treatments I would receive—many of which I was trained in. Their clinicians used EMDR and Internal Family Systems (IFS), a model that helps clients explore different "parts" of their emotional makeup.

Dr. G. also explained I would experience therapies less familiar to me, like brainspotting (another type of brain stimulation therapy that uses the optic nerve combined with music), psychodrama (the re-creation of poignant moments with members of group therapy playing the characters of your life, so as to rescript the outcome), breath work (a powerful breathing process combined with music that activates the calming systems of the brain), equine therapy, and, if the weather cooperated, possibly a sweat lodge.

"I'm open to anything," I said with a slight pulse of energy.

He declared this combo of treatments my best hope for getting well.

I concentrated on Dr. G.'s face but lost focus every few words. I watched a bread crumb perched above his mouth bounce up and down on his beard as he spoke. I was soothed to have found another place for my thoughts to rest. A version of myself would have alerted the kind doctor to the crumb, but I could not summon her. I exhaled in the relief of admitting the depth of my illness. I felt flickers of strong desire to get well and little or no resistance to any suggestion made on my behalf.

As the doctor and I ambled in the Tennessee heat, I felt bubbles of hope beginning to rise in my chest. I was eager to participate in my healing but knew I should not be in charge of it. Trusting myself to be just a patient would take some getting used to; it was still hard to wrap my head around the fact that I was no longer sitting in a therapist's chair. I'd long identified myself by my roles—helper, caregiver, wife, and mom. It was wildly disorienting to have to concede them all and be a client.

"We've diagnosed you with C-PTSD, depression, and anxiety." Dr. G. paused to let his words sink in. It was a relief to hear him state my illnesses so plainly, like named problems that could be matched with solutions.

As if reading my mind, he continued. "Your case is particularly severe because of the compound trauma of childhood loss and the successive deaths of your parents. Your mother's was so unexpected . . ." His voice trailed off. We walked for a moment in silence. "Do you think you went into freeze?" he asked gently.

Most people consider our defensive instincts—fight, flight, and freeze—to be equal, but even addled, my brain knew the body protects itself best when it can offer some sort of resistance to a trauma. When terror and fear freeze in the body, it can leave it traumatized. A person may survive but find themselves easily overwhelmed and on guard against any future attacks. Persistent anxiety often sets up residence inside the house.

I nodded through the tears that seemed so persistent recently.

"No wonder it's been so bad." Dr G.'s southern twang was genuinely filled with empathy. "Your report says your symptoms are a nineteen out of twenty." He referenced the PTSD checklist we both knew and used. Nineteen might have been normal for inpatient, but I'd never treated anyone higher than a fifteen. I nodded and clenched my jaw against the picture of my mother's dead body that had again begun to swirl.

We walked an easy minute in silence before I found myself saying, "My mother had PTSD when I was a kid."

Dr. G. nodded thoughtfully, looking down at his feet. "Trauma can be handed down," he replied. After a minute he asked, "What's your memory like?"

Did he mean traumatic memory? I thought of how the smell of sunscreen could bring me back to the sound of my oldest brother's panicked voice yelling for our mother.

I sighed heavily and replied, "It used to be abnormally good. Particularly visual." Dr. G. nodded and encouraged me to continue. "If you told me the name of your childhood dog, I'd remember it *and* the color of the sweater you were wearing when you told me." Dr. G. chuckled. "Never the dates of the Civil War... numbers not so much," I clarified.

Dr. G. smiled. "Well, I know you know this"—it was the only time he referenced my pedigrees—"but women and people with good memories are more susceptible to PTSD. That's you, twice over." I wasn't sure I'd learned those correlations before but took them as permission to consider dropping a few of the sticks I'd been using in my self-flagellation.

I thought back to the answers I'd given to the questions about my PTSD symptoms during my intake the previous day. Did I:

Have nightmares or thoughts about the events when I
    did not want to?
Try hard not to think about the events or go out of my
    way to avoid situations that reminded me of
    them?
Find myself constantly on guard, watchful, or easily
    startled?
Feel numb or detached from people, activities, or my
    surroundings?
Have upsetting thoughts or memories about the events
    come into my mind against my will?
Have body sensations like a rapid heartbeat, nausea,
    sweating, and dizziness when reminded of the events?
Have feelings of guilt?
Constantly blame myself?

It was as though the survey had been written *about* me. The guilt was the worst. I felt handcuffed like a criminal who was constantly reminded of the details of her crime. I hadn't insisted on more medical care. I hadn't checked on her more frequently. I did not go closer, though I knew she was ill and hardly eating.

As if reading my mind, Dr. G. asked, "How are you feeling right now?" He sounded concerned.

I paused for a moment, trying to summon a true answer. "I'm not sure I can feel anything." The words rushed out in one gasp. "I don't know who I am anymore. I have no idea what I am even doing here." I gulped a hiccup.

Dr. G. waited for me to stop crying and handed me a tissue that seemed to materialize out of nowhere. "It's my understanding you asked for help. You got yourself here. *You* did that, didn't you?" His voice was low and kind in an unfamiliar fatherly way.

I felt the significance of what adult support could mean to a traumatized child.

"I did do that." He held open the proverbial door and encouraged me to take a tiny step.

In childhood I'd made do with what was available, not allowing myself to need more. But I *had* needed help. I'd spent years in therapy coming to understand that the crappy umbrella I'd created of helping and hiding had never really kept me out of the storm. A part of me was furious to discover I still had no coverage after all these years.

"You became a helper." Dr. G. bestowed the words like a formal title—a quick reminder of who I was, my purpose, and my definition. "And this time, you helped yourself."

For a split second, I felt an odd swell of gratitude. I thought of all the times I'd been on the receiving end of a client's thanks as we ended our hour together. I'd always wanted them to understand my therapist job was more like a midwife to the work they did to heal. Standing in front of Dr. G., his voice so filled with confidence, I felt a little less lost.

The moment of peace left as quickly as it came, replaced again by the images and crushing judgment that leveled me anytime my mind was distracted by other thoughts.

It is your fault she died. It is your fault you are sick.

I had seen ruminations relentlessly torture my clients. Neither theirs nor mine told the truth, but knowing that did not stop them. I was relieved when Dr. G. interrupted my brutal internal dialogue again with "You will heal. It just takes time." I noticed his T-shirt with the center's motto, "Trust the Process," emblazoned across the chest. I did trust it, but frankly, what choice did I have? My brain flickered with the faces of my clients whom I'd had the honor of working alongside as they fought so hard to get well. Had I abandoned them to save myself? It was hard to see past my own pain to even think of them at all.

In our hour-and-a-half-long walking meeting, Dr. G. never deferred to me. For that, I was incredibly grateful. He was in charge. He suggested a blood pressure medication I'd vaguely heard of that had the added side effect of dispelling traumatic images from sleep. I immediately agreed and decided not to do my own research or ask for a second opinion.

"You are going to do a lot of therapy here," Dr. G. said. He pointed back toward the building from where we'd just come. I was startled to see it was much closer than it felt. "Just like everyone else, you are going to have to figure out how to show up for the unresolved pain of your childhood as well as your present loss with all the courage and resources you have as an adult." I sighed audibly. I knew this work intimately both as a therapist and as a client. I also knew it could be grueling.

"I've done a lot of inner-child work already," I half moaned.

"Yep. And you are going to do a whole bunch more." Dr. G. patted my shoulder warmly.

Before we parted at the door, he turned to me and said in a stern doctor's tone: "The therapy is important, but so is the time away from anything that competes for your attention—work, family, *especially* your kids. The only person you need to take care of right now is you. Anything else will undermine your healing."

It was as though Dr. G. had pulled off all my invisible name tags and replaced them instead with "DAUGHTER" written in bold block letters. I felt the opposite of shame. I felt seen and grateful. The fear of losing other parts of me—wife, mother—lingered but was no match for the relief I felt at being told to temporarily step out of those roles. I walked toward the rest of my day seeing glimmers of hope glinting out of the corner of my eye.

THIRTY

There was a small hill ahead of me that I'd have to climb to get to equine therapy. The problem was, I had zero energy to do so. Nor did I want to.

The forty-five-year-old therapist part of me vaguely remembered learning that low muscle tone is a common feature of active trauma. So is general pain and weakness. Just after my father's funeral, I had dragged my body across a crowded airport with neither the physical strength nor the mental clarity to make it to the gate. Mike saved me by flagging down the mobility cart. My three children were delighted by the unexpected ride.

On the ranch, my knight in shining armor took the shape of a man named Dave who appeared at my side in a golf cart. He had zipped over from around the side of the building as if anticipating my falter.

Most staff at Foundations had job titles with initials like CA (client assistant) and were all "here to help." Dave, who eventually ferried me to the horse paddock at the top of the hill, was a CA with a bum knee. He graciously pretended I'd given him an excuse not to walk the hill himself, but I noticed later that the staff ran a golf cart a minute or two behind most newcomers.

My nose took in the sweet, familiar smells of hay, leather, and manure as Dave dropped me as close to the stables as the cart would allow. Other clients were seated in Adirondack chairs. They seemed to be circled around an imaginary fire. One or two people had stepped into the meadow and were affectionally nuzzling horses they seemed to know by name. I sat down in mild irritation. I'd grown up riding horses and read clinical books on equine therapy. I really wasn't an animal person and did not have high expectations for the next hour.

As a kid, I rode at a stable that was more L.L.Bean duck shoes and jeans than fancy leather boots and jodhpurs. Because of my pathological people-pleasing, I regularly said yes to being paired with a giant horse named Misty who was prone to stopping short at jumps and whom no one else wanted to ride. If I had stopped to think about the thirty dollars (not a small sum back then) my mother paid for the lessons I did not want, I still wouldn't have spoken up. Either way, I would have been plagued by guilt.

As I stood there awkwardly, I thought of a past client who had described her experience with equine therapy as her most powerful modality of healing. "It's beyond words," she gushed. I responded by giving her a lecture on how the brains of some animals (dogs, cats, wolves, horses) allow intuitive connection with humans in ways our critical-thinking frontal lobes often prevent with each other. "My horse took care of me," my client reported. I remembered being dubious but grateful that she felt that way.

"Okay people, let's circle up." Our instructor's voice was vaguely familiar as she strode out of the barn with purpose. I also recognized the cowboy boots and hat but could not place the face. "Who's new?" she asked, and I started to feel dizzy. She then stepped near and reached for a large black bucket filled with stiff-bristled brushes.

"You're new," my roommate whispered in my direction. It took a minute to understand that meant I should raise my hand. "She's new," Rachel finally offered on my behalf. The cowgirl walked toward me with a smile that clouded as she approached.

"Hey…" She drew out her steps and her speech, cocking her head at me with uncertain recognition.

"Hey?" It was clear we knew each other. My mind offered me all the places where we might have met: church, work, supermarket, post office, charity, school…

"Labyrinth," Maggie finally exhaled with a smile. "I've never forgotten that day. God, it was raining." She swept me into a swift hug, adding, "I'm so glad you're here." My mind struggled to keep up.

My face betrayed that I could barely discern the past from the present.

"I used to work there," Maggie offered simply, referring to the other treatment center where we'd first met. "Now I work here." I nodded, my memory sharpening. "It was your dad, right?" She squinted in the sun.

"Actually, my mom this time," I replied. I felt both relieved and oddly exposed finding someone from another time and place here with me now. "Take a brush," she said without offering platitudes. She continued to walk the imaginary campfire circle of seated clients, handing a brush to each one.

The clients took their brushes and walked comfortably into the training ring. Each selected a horse while Maggie ushered me into a chair. I couldn't formulate my questions about our last encounter, so instead I answered Maggie's. No, I wasn't afraid of horses; yes, I could ride; no, I didn't want to. She told me the names of the six animals in the ring and how they'd come to the ranch. Each had a history of mistreatment. "They need love just as much as you do," Maggie offered softly.

She walked me into the ring, where she called to the rest of the group, "Let's switch." All brushing stopped, and the group turned toward us. "Let Meghan and her horse find each other first."

The other clients receded to the outside ring, as I stood small and obscured in an equine sea. In a previous life I would have felt self-conscious. In this one, I was too irritated and exhausted. I watched a horse amble over to a tall wooden post, dip her head, and begin scratching vigorously. I found myself staring.

"Go to the horse you feel drawn to," Maggie instructed. "Don't overthink it."

I walked toward the scratching horse, neither the most beautiful nor the most imposing. I felt jealous of her self-centeredness. I was oddly rooting for her. "That's Dagger," a nearby voice told me, and I felt my face break open with an unfamiliar smile at the ridiculous incongruence of her name. The horse seemed dopey and gentle and as though she belonged very much to herself. She was nobody's weapon. As I moved closer, I felt the slight movements of the other horses as they found partners in other clients. It was as if we were part of a well-orchestrated dance.

"What am I supposed to do?" I asked quietly, but loud enough that my annoyed tone reached the two women on either side of me. I was always short on patience when I felt confused.

"Just brush her," one answered. "Whatever feels right," the other said.

I felt a quick burst of the anger that erupted more frequently these days. Nothing felt right. *Why should I brush this fucking horse?* Equine therapy was bullshit, and I needed real help. My frustrated tears puffed in the dust as they fell at my feet.

Dagger moved on my right, and instinctively I moved slightly left. She stepped toward me again; I stepped away again.

"Be conscious of the conversation you are having with your horse." Maggie's comment seemed obviously directed at me.

I tested myself, standing still as the horse stepped closer, then again and again. Slowly, almost in micromovements, Dagger aligned the sway of her back right under my chin. I didn't move, but soon our bodies were almost touching in a T shape. Though her mini-steps felt odd, my mind was not curious.

"Do what feels natural," Maggie coached. My instinct, as always, was to look around to see what others were doing—as if they might have my answer. Out of the corner of my eye I could see Maggie working with a young man who had curly hair and shaking hands.

What felt natural was exhaustion, what felt right was resting my forehead down onto Dagger's back, which was inexplicably right in front of me. When I look back on the moment, I'm grateful that the brain shuts parts of itself down in trauma. If I'd been more clearheaded, I would have walked out of the ring.

Dagger shuddered with what felt like a sigh and swished her tail as I laid my forehead on her soft, glossy back. She shimmied, causing my head to rest more heavily and fully on her. Within two minutes, Dagger had contorted her shape until she was supporting the whole weight of me, and I inexplicably began to yawn as though I might fall asleep.

"Do what feels natural," I heard Maggie say again. It was still annoying, but I listened. I extended my arms out wide to keep myself supported. I kept leaning on Dagger and allowed my eyes to close. I worked my hands in small circles through her coarse coat, scratching her gently underneath. The fibrous texture on my fingers grounded me in the present. It felt as though someone had turned on a dim light inside my head, just behind my eyes. My chest inflated ever so slightly, starting to warm and open a bit where a moment ago it had been filled with only thick, metallic heaviness.

Rubbing Dagger, I had an odd memory of running my hands across one of my mother's area rugs as a child. But perhaps it wasn't odd. The brain catalogs like experiences together. Even then, the rough fibers had soothed me. Later I would think of this moment and be reminded that bilateral movement—using both sides of the body—can offer balance to an overstimulated brain. It allowed me to appreciate my instincts as a child, even if my efforts weren't quite enough.

"What do you feel?" Suddenly, Maggie was at my side. I kept my eyes closed, searching inside my dark body for an answer. My thoughts swept out as though by a strong wind. My mind suddenly offered new words: "It's going to be okay." I felt the small light return and expand past my chest, into my arms and legs. Maggie put her hand on my back, and I wondered for a second if it might be best described as "hope." I said the word out loud.

"Funny how sometimes all you have to do is lean into it," Maggie offered warmly. She instructed us all to take a few breaths and to "say thank you to your horse." I popped my eyes open with a newfound energy. I swept around to look Dagger in the face and rubbed the long, hard bone between her eyes. I felt alert. Electricity tingled beneath my skin.

In past therapy, I'd learned to grieve. With my hand still on Dagger's face, I now contemplated my thoughts about being unsupported in childhood. Couldn't my parents have helped me? Wouldn't they have at least tried? What if my long-term childhood trauma was more about never learning how to ask for help and less on account of it not being available?

I heard my own voice repeating a therapist favorite: "Feelings are not facts."

I'd felt helpless and alone in grief as a child. I felt helpless and alone in grief as an adult.

No one is coming to save me but me.

But I was coming to understand that didn't mean it had to be me alone.

The light in my chest remained. The way down the hill was easier than the way up.

· · ·

My therapist Jo was older than me by at least a decade. She wore heavy clogs and a no-nonsense kind of smile that I liked immediately. Rachel told me Jo was admired as much for her clinical skills as for her T-shirt collection. Today's was a frayed putty color shirt that read "Earth Day, Berkeley 2000." The faded retro design was almost completely covered by a giant necklace made of multicolored beads that resembled sea glass.

I settled into the sofa across from where she sat in her over-sized purple velvet chair. It would take me a few sessions to place it, but the decor and color scheme of Jo's office reminded me of a children's television show starring singing dogs that my kids had been obsessed with—hand puppets in bright yellows and electric blues.

I spent our first meeting trying to quickly share the high-lights of my oft-told timeline. Occasionally, she stopped me.

"What do you mean you were a bridesmaid *eight* times?" Jo asked. I had casually mentioned I'd spent most of my time and all of my money one summer in my twenties going to eleven weddings, eight of which I was in. "Did you have eight brides-maids?" she asked incredulously. I shook my head and barked a laugh. She followed up with what I would come to think of as one of her signature record scratchers: "Any idea why so many women felt closer to you than you did to them?" For a moment I wondered if the question was rhetorical.

"It's safer to have lots of friends," I finally whispered into the silence that had hung between us for a solid minute.

"It isn't, actually," Jo said. She sounded like she felt sorry for me. "Needs do not make you a liability, Meghan. Just human."

I wondered if I had been paying dues in relationships,

always eyeing the lifeboats, prepping for calamity. I'd kept my relationship circle large and loose, forgetting that the purpose of friendship was to feel connected, not indebted.

Every session, Jo chipped away at the brutal images of my mother's death that had been making it nearly impossible for me to sleep. The work was slow but relieving.

In an early session, Jo handed me a pen and notebook. "Write the worst of it," she said. "Write it like a story."

Much like a mixtape, my mind had a hit list of "horror images" that were in constant rotation: the parking lot, the idling minivan, Mike's tearstained face, her hands and feet. Her hands and feet bordered on intolerable.

Jo explained she planned to use EMDR, the trauma treatment that Dr. G. had referred to in our initial meeting. I had been in therapy for years before I even understood what EMDR was. Now I could hardly recall how I had done trauma work without it. In my experience EMDR could occasionally diffuse intense memories in the very first session.

When I put down my pen after nearly a half hour of writing, Jo said, "Read it to me."

My voice shook as I recounted driving up to the house and seeing the police car. How I'd hugged Mike and understood immediately that he would never tell me what these hours had been like for him. How I repeatedly moaned "I can't do this" as he kept me from falling.

"Let's work here," Jo interrupted. She took my notebook and replaced it with the EMDR tappers. Her voice floated like a gentle voice-over into my memory.

"Close your eyes and picture the scene you just described."

I took a deep breath.

"Nod when you can feel yourself back in that moment."

In my imagination, I saw the stones of the driveway, felt the light rain, heard the caw of seagulls, and smelled the pine and salt. I nodded slowly.

"Now ask yourself this question: What or who can help me here?" Jo instructed and turned on the tappers, which immediately began buzzing from one palm to the other. The images came alive like a scene in a movie I'd seen a million times. But this time, like a choose-your-own-adventure book from my childhood, my imagination offered me an alternate ending.

My memory picked up where Jo had paused the story. I watched myself step out of Mike's hug and noticed a new person calmly standing to his left. She had not been there in real life. It took me a second to recognize her.

It was me.

I was standing next to my husband—my hair a little longer, hips thicker, eyes creased with age.

And I was a force.

Still whispering, "I can't, I can't, I can't," like an incantation or a blessing, the me who had yet to live through the trauma stepped next to the woman who already had. I looked right into my own terrified, wild, heartsick eyes.

Like the women warriors of the Māori, the me of the present and the me of the future leaned forehead-to-forehead, nose-to-nose, breath-to-breath. No words passed between us. We stared into each other's eyes and then embraced, clutching and desperate, almost too tight. The offer was for courage and company only. There would be no rescue here. The chant transformed from "I can't" to "I will," then "I am." I was no longer alone.

The tappers buzzed. The shift took only seconds. I watched myself turn and walk up the steps of my parents' house, knowing what I would find inside, humbled that I would go in anyway. When Jo turned off the tappers, I knew I would never live that moment or the memory of it without myself again.

THIRTY-ONE

My treatment plan included the written directive that I should seek out others when images of death woke me in the middle of the night. Like a little girl looking for her parents after waking with a nightmare, I sought out company.

Even at 3:00 a.m., someone was always awake: staff or other clients. I would slip out of my room, quietly close the door, and tiptoe to the common area, where I was regularly greeted by a small clutch of night owls fighting their own late-night demons. For them, my wee-hour wanderings barely piqued curiosity. No one suggested warm milk or meditation, or offered a personal success story of curing themselves with melatonin. A lot of trauma work was just scooching over on the couch to give each other room to sit.

Sleeplessness was a primary complaint from many of my grieving clients. I hadn't ever fully understood just how an embodied lack of sleep infects every aspect of one's ability to function. Sure, I'd been a sleep-deprived parent to a newborn, but I'd saved myself by napping. Grief insomnia was a secondary loss. My perpetual exhaustion meant I was edgy and spongelike, absorbing every small hurt.

The first time I wandered into the common area at night, I sat, listening in on a surreal conversation about where the small subset of clients, all far younger than me, skied each winter. Names of fancy hotels and resorts I'd never heard of were volleyed back and forth in a way that was both intriguing and off-putting.

"We go to Utah," one man explained to heads that nodded as I wondered who the "we" was. Earlier in the day, I heard him refer to an incredibly expensive SUV as "our car" only to discover he meant his father's car. I didn't stop myself from asking him how old he was.

"Just turned thirty," he said forthrightly. In the coming weeks I would meet several more clients in their midtwenties and early thirties who were raised in extreme wealth. Each of their complex stories made sense to me, but I couldn't help wondering if all that money might have caused some of the very problems it was expected to solve.

Things I had referred to as a hardship in other times of my life—college waitressing jobs, grad school loans, no money for a group trip to Mexico—had also helped me establish the hustle that drove my confidence to separate from my family, however awkwardly I may have managed it. My father walked a fine line between supporting and not coddling his children financially. More than once, I wondered whether he felt more pride or envy that his hard-earned financial success had given us a security he'd never had growing up. I wouldn't have blamed him for either.

For the most part, the treatment center's late-night crew were people I profoundly liked but rarely had a chance to spend time with during the day. There was often a male duo playing chess in one corner of the great room. Up in the art loft, the insomniac painter from Turkey could be found blending swaths of vibrant colors on a large canvas. A tiny, angry young woman named Isla, whose recent medication change had upset her serotonin levels, sat on the floor hunched over the coffee table. Her long, unwashed hair hung in curtains as she drew complicated anime figures that looked impossibly computer generated. As generous as she was furious, Isla would give me an almost imperceptible nod before pulling a page off her heavyweight art pad and holding it straight up for me to take. At her feet sat a tackle box of expensive, dual-tipped pens that off-gassed in such a way I was surprised they hadn't been confiscated at the door.

Almost thirty years my junior, Isla had thin arms that were marked with wounds she likely caused herself. I felt calmer when I sat close to her genius and pain. Sometimes I even allowed myself to make long, soothing lines with her pens, imagining the ink represented sorrow that I carved out of me and left on the paper instead.

"Do you have pictures running through your head?" The question came from a young woman who'd been married only twenty-five days before her mind began to unfurl memories of sexual abuse from early childhood. She was still in her wedding gown when the compulsive vomiting started.

I was startled that she'd noticed me at all on the late-night couch.

"I pretty much always do, at night," I answered honestly.

She did not shy away. "Is it a still picture or a movie?" Her expanded question felt as though she was asking about a specific street in the town where we'd both grown up.

"It's more like a flip-book," I responded, without pausing to check my audience. Back home, I'd made a habit of first deciding how much of my chaos was okay to share. As a therapist, I had been trained not to ask about a rumination in this level of detail, but I found it comforting now.

"Tell me," she said.

"I see her long fingers still wrapped in a rosary; her blue heel pulled back from the duvet where someone tried to get her pulse. I see myself covering her hands and feet before my brother comes in. I see a smattering of light through the curtains that send small triangles across her body in a way that makes it almost seem like she's still moving."

Describing the images out loud ejected them from my mind for a few minutes.

"Oh yeah . . ." Isla groaned from her place at the table. She lifted her head and swept her hair back so her gray eyes and heavy lashes were visible. "I actually made a book of the pictures I saw in my head." She clicked her tongue in emphasis. "That didn't go over well. My mom called the head doctor, said it was a cry for help."

"Was it?" an unseen voice called out from the loft. The painter was at a distance but still connected to the conversation from above. Isla sunk her head back to her drawing. "I don't know. But I felt better. I can tell you that. I stayed up for three days straight drawing the pictures out of my mind. I didn't have to think them anymore. Then I slept for a whole week."

"That makes a lot of sense, actually," I said, wishing I knew how to draw.

"Yeah. The best part was the shrink told my mom that my drawings were a healthy processing tool—not morbid or sick." Isla flashed a perfect smile that suggested years of orthodontics. "My mom had already burned my book by that point, though, so that sucked."

A week later I learned from Isla that she and her best friend had been in a car accident that had killed another driver. On the first anniversary, her friend, who had been charged with causing the accident, swallowed a fatal dose of sedatives and drove into a nearby lake and died.

The "nighthawks" made it easy to challenge my habit of hide-and-retreat. They helped me practice a calm and slow monitoring of my panic level. If it got too high, we would decide collectively to ask a clinical staff member to help. One of the legacies of trauma is not being able to judge when you become overwhelmed. I was amazed at how truly relieving depending on other people, even those fighting their own battles, could feel.

In the daylight hours, food remained a challenge. I was almost never hungry despite the gorgeous buffet-style meals cooked for us daily. The first time the busy kitchen staff made deliberate efforts to include one of my favorite foods, I cried at both the thoughtfulness of being considered and the knowledge I would not be able to eat it.

When I was a child, my mother cooked with green peppers, a vegetable I would later learn caused me consistent heartburn and nausea. I didn't have the vocabulary to explain why I rarely liked my mother's cooking, but my discomfort eventually earned me the description of "picky," which was terrible when all I wanted was to be accommodating. Like most labels given to me by someone else, I quickly internalized it. In a family of six kids, I never expected my mother to take my food preferences into account, nor did she.

After a few days in treatment, the kind chef, Chase, pulled me aside to ask if I thought I might be able to handle a smoothie. "Maybe," I replied, and he blended me a green concoction based on a recipe I often made at home. "There is pretty much nothing we won't try to help you get well," he said when I thanked him. I blushed, wondering if I could say the same.

It reminded me of advice I'd once heard from a supervising therapist: "Never work harder than your clients."

That afternoon, I tried the soup option at lunch. I managed only a few bites of the cauliflower cream drizzled with truffle oil, but by the end of the week, I'd worked my way up to a whole bowl.

THIRTY-TWO

One cool evening, as the kitchen was closing, there was a verified rumor of a possible outing to Dairy Queen running through the halls. It seemed certain staff were susceptible to being sweet-talked into short field trips. The excitement was palpable. I knew I shouldn't stay behind on my own. We piled into minivans, and I sat toward the back, off to the side.

A well-loved CA drove the fifteen minutes to Dairy Queen, where twenty or so of us tumbled out of the vans and into the parking lot. With bashful giggling and bursts of shoving and running, we might have been mistaken for a church group on our way back from a volunteer project.

Our members formed a line, but I found the sight of the soft serve repellent. I slid into a red molded plastic bench at a table meant for four and was quickly joined by Crystal and Gail. They were both in treatment for more than a month, and Dairy

Queen was old news to them. They'd come for the change of scenery, they insisted. Their conversation seemed stilted in that way that sometimes happens when people who know each other well in one environment find themselves in a far different one.

My concentration dipped in and out until a childhood memory of Dairy Queen floated to the surface: A kind middle school soccer coach had once taken me and his own kids out for ice cream after a particularly brutal loss. My parents' weekends were occasionally split among my brothers' various sports, which meant they not only missed my games but also often asked my coach, who lived in our same town, to bring me back and forth. The coach's daughter, Noelle, had long legs, long hair, and long nails. She was beloved by the clutch of sixth-grade girls who made up our team. Popular and a high scorer, she was never anything but completely kind to me. I often wondered if she ever suspected I was jealous of everything about her, including her attentive father, who had wanted to spend time with her so much he became the coach.

The stop at Dairy Queen was almost certainly for me. I was the team's goalie, more out of willingness than skill, and I'd let in a variety of easy saves. Despite Noelle scoring a hat trick, my poor performance had led us to a humiliating defeat.

Noelle and her older brother, Jack, were Dairy Queen regulars and knew their ice-cream orders without even glancing at the menu. It was my first time. The short line didn't allow for much decision-making, so I impulsively asked for a variation on their orders, which I'd heard to be ice cream with syrup. The teenage clerk repeated my order back to me and I nodded with confidence.

Jack and Noelle's small white cream twists dripping in caramel came in shallow Styrofoam saucers. When the clerk reached around for my order, I gasped audibly. Twice the size of the others, mine came in a mini navy-blue Boston Red Sox hard helmet.

My shock was obvious, and I took the cup in near tears, to which the teenager replied unkindly, "I asked you." I was mortified by both the size and cost of the treat. I apologized to my coach for my gaffe, though he seemed genuinely nonplussed. I insisted on doubling down in shame by comparing my larger-sized body to that of Noelle and other girls on the team. I assumed my coach and his family were secretly judging me.

Once back in the car, I took one bite of the sickeningly sweet dessert and wished I'd agreed to go to my brother's tournament rather than insisting on letting my team down. We drove home to the sound of Madonna on the radio while the vanilla and golden syrup melted into soup in my cup. I spent the entire ride holding the cap impossibly steady so as not to spill it on the soft maroon seats of the clean station wagon. Instead, I spilled it down the entirety of my bright yellow polyester goalie shirt as I exited the car onto my driveway. Fake laughing and waving a smile of thanks, I opened the house's big blue door and pretended to call to my parents, who I knew were not at home.

Still alone hours later, I washed my shirt by hand in the bathroom sink to avoid explaining what a mistake I was to my mother and made myself a large bowl of ice cream from our freezer for dinner.

I wondered if my reluctance toward the ice cream now had anything to do with my oddly specific memory. The lingering loneliness of my childhood mixed with the shame of the old belief that people would reject me for being myself. I heard my own therapist voice saying, *We are rarely truly doing anything for the first time. Most behaviors are built on past experiences and the meaning we make from them.* I wondered whether my lifelong avoidance of Dairy Queen came from the belief that they served crappy ice cream or the belief that I was a crappy kid.

At some point during the ice-cream ordering and serving, a member of our group, Andy, slid into our booth and casually mentioned that his milkshake had somehow been missed in the chaos. He seemed not to care, but I found myself distracted. I could almost see myself walk to the counter with my recently lost charm, explain the mistake, get an upgrade on the frozen treat, and earn the admiration and gratitude of those watching.

Almost like a vision, I watched an old version of myself walk out the door, but I did not move until we were called back to the vans.

No phone calls were allowed for the first five days in treatment. By the time new clients received phone privileges, the calls home were usually quite emotional. Right after dinner, the common area would become a complicated waiting list of clients hoping to talk to loved ones. Most people used one of the two old-school push-button landlines that were set up in the corners of the great room. Parents were given permission for extra-long video calls with their children in a private room, which often led to tears on all sides. As Dr. G. had suggested, my treatment plan made clear that would not be the case for me. My phone calls were kept to fifteen minutes exactly—five minutes per kid and just a quick hello to my husband, no video.

The first time I punched in Mike's cell number, my hands shook. I anticipated pain on both sides of the phone line.

The kids surprised me with their cheery, very kid-like excited selves. Instead of worries, they had questions.

"Is it a one- or a two-man bed?" Daniel wanted to know.

"Two, but I'm alone in it." I chuckled.

"Have you had any ice cream?" Nicky asked.

"Not yet, but they did take us out for soft serve," I answered, smiling. Like heat-seeking missiles, my kids looked for the good.

"How many dogs are there?" Lucy seemed intrigued by the idea of animals.

"Two. They have very different personalities, which is fun."

Mike reassured me that everyone was well and that I was missed. The familiar ease in his voice brought tears to my eyes. But I did not miss them back—not yet. There were still layers of lingering guilt I needed to excavate myself from before I could rediscover the "I" who got to do the missing in the first place. The faraway voices that called "I love you" down the phone made my chest expand. I hung up wondering if I was the kind of mother who sacrificed everything for her kids. And what was the definition of "everything"?

THIRTY-THREE

The residential staff checked in regularly. How were our calls home? Did we need any materials for art assignments? A run to Target over the weekend? How about Sunday church service?

The idea of church intrigued me. I'd been without spiritual country or congregation for a few years, but the craving to belong to something bigger persisted. I added my name to the list.

As a child I'd mostly enjoyed church. I liked the ritual of standing, kneeling, reciting, and singing, and I found the stories from the Bible fascinating. The Old Testament with its floods and famines, the New Testament with impossibly hard-to-believe reports of a man who walked on water and turned water into wine. It seemed unwise to take the whole Book literally, but the plotlines, akin to Greek mythology, often had me tingling.

Early every Sunday morning of my childhood—no jeans, no sneakers—we caravanned to a church several towns and socio-economic degrees away from our house, where my family took up an entire pew. My siblings and I mostly sat still during Mass while we dug pens out of my mother's purse and drew on the pages of the bulletin. I always listened, though I pretended I didn't.

I must have been under ten when I first heard the phrase "To whom much is given, much is expected" (a paraphrase of Luke 12:48). I understood the message implicitly. Looking around at the congregation full of families, all of whom seemed to have less than ours, I understood we were the "to whom much is given." I never could work out if it was devotion, obedience, or money that I owed.

On Sunday morning, I gathered with the churchgoers in the main lobby before clambering into the van for the half-hour ride off campus. Our driver, Holly, my favorite among the Foundations staff, answered some general programming questions about the week ahead on our otherwise quiet drive.

"We have a guest speaker at the AA meeting on Tuesday," she offered. "I won't say who, but he's from country music." With its proximity to Nashville, Foundations had a deep connection to the music community.

"How come you don't go to meetings?" The question came from Corey, a man about my age, who had checked in the same day I did. He was quiet and kept mostly to himself. His direct question startled me.

"I'm not an alcoholic," I said flatly, and then qualified my statement with "but only because I don't drink much." I realized how ridiculous the words sounded as they left my mouth.

"No addictions at all?" His mouth crooked into a smile. Just because I wasn't working a recovery program didn't mean I was living sober. Everyone in the van knew the likelihood of finding yourself in a trauma facility and not having some dysfunctional escapist behavior was unlikely.

"Food is more of a problem. Or has been. Or is. I can't tell. I've sort of stopped eating, but I can definitely binge. I used to exercise too much, shopping, TV, and I recently learned isolating can be an addiction, so . . ." I let my voice trail off, unsure why I seemed to be trying to gain his acceptance.

Corey nodded almost as though in approval, and I was reminded of the quick sense of panic I felt watching most of the center's clients pile into the main room for the 8:00 p.m. AA meeting without me. Many of my favorite people were sober. My desire to belong was so great, it seemed I didn't care what I belonged to.

"I'm more process addiction myself," Jennifer offered, breaking the awkward silence. "I'm not much of a drinker," she continued, "but boy can I do some damage shopping or playing poker online." A decade older than me, she still managed to project a youthful homecoming queen's poise and pep. She gave me a broad smile, and her eyes sparkled. "I'm always wrestling one of those demons," she said with her pretty southern twang.

Holly pulled into the parking lot of what looked like a strip mall anchored by a giant sporting goods store. It took me a minute to understand the building *was* the church. No white clapboards, no steeple, just people dressed in khakis, polos, and an occasional cowboy boot streaming into the warehouse. I'd heard of megachurches held in movie theaters or closed stores on weekends, but I'd never been to one. I climbed down from the van feeling grateful I would not have to decide if I should report this back to my parents.

We stepped through the doors, and the sound hit instantly. The nearby Nashville influence had leveled up the praise music. Just inside the main door, the band looked like they were headlining a full-fledged rock concert with a drummer, a bassist, a lead guitarist, and three extraordinary singers belting out tight three-part harmony. I had to listen closely to hear the occasional "Jesus" lyric as a clue we were actually at church.

As I approached the main entrance, people clustered to the right, picking up a small item from a tray I couldn't quite see. Out of curiosity or peer pressure, I took one, thinking it might be a candle, and stepped into the main room now cloaked in concert darkness.

The music picked up again, as did the lights, and I looked down at the small item in my hand. Shaped like a diner coffee creamer shot, it took me a moment to make sense of the tiny plastic cup of red liquid topped with a foil liner that held a small circular cracker in place. It was the Eucharist: the body and blood of Christ in a single-serving to-go cup. When the reenactment of the Last Supper came, hundreds of people simultaneously cracked open the plastic containers, creating a room-wide whispering crackle that made me glad I'd come. An hour later our group walked back out of the darkness into the Tennessee heat with songs of praise and the promise of salvation behind us.

As we climbed back into the van, I felt the disappointment of knowing that whatever answer I was looking for, it wasn't in church. I had been promised this form of salvation before. I knew I'd come seeking something impossible—a map back to a life that no longer existed. I needed compassion, I needed to grieve, but I did not need to be saved.

THIRTY-FOUR

I was finally sleeping and eating more regularly, which meant I qualified for the equivalent of treatment "recess" known as "outdoor adventure." Classes were compulsory and led by Billy, a tree-loving therapist with a strong goofy side. Larger than life, and quick to laughter or tears, Billy reminded me ever so slightly of Hagrid from the Harry Potter franchise.

Many of the longer-term clients were already familiar with Billy's outdoor education series and the requisite trust fall (off a four-foot porch to make it that much more terrifying). I'd managed to evade trust falls in the past and was beginning to calculate if I wanted to resist or comply when I found Billy at my elbow.

"I'm doing this for you," he said softly. "We all are. Everyone here has already found a way to fall safely." I noted his choice of words.

Obviously, I had no choice. I silently stood at the precipice of the porch. I didn't shake or cry, but I also couldn't let myself let go. Minutes ticked by. Eventually a professional athlete who was becoming a friend pulled away from the group. He looked me straight in the eye and pointed meaningfully, then he leaned forward and whispered in my ear, "I've got you. I will not drop you. I can catch you myself, but I'm going to let these guys think they helped." He glanced over his shoulder at our group's arms zippered in formation, waiting to make the catch. He gave me a broad smile as he sauntered back to his place. I took one more deep breath, clutched my fear, closed my eyes, and fell.

A quick wash of adrenaline rushed through me as I noticed the effort it took to hold my weight. I felt an old fleeting sense of shame at my size, but it was quickly supplanted by gratitude for the hands underneath and around me, holding me up in my powerlessness. My cheeks warmed with pride at being able to check off another "thing I will try in order to get well." When my feet were guided back to the ground, I found myself nose-to-nose with a dozen smiling faces and a physical understanding of what it truly means to put yourself in the hands of others.

The following Tuesday, Billy broke our larger group of twenty-one into two. Half went into the woods with another instructor while my collection of eleven followed Billy up the hill to a large Huck Finn sort of plank raft. It was set across a large roller that ran down the middle, creating a giant teeter-totter akin to a child's seesaw.

Billy explained the rules carefully. In as few minutes as possible, our challenge was to get the entire group on the raft, balancing precisely so the edges didn't touch the ground. Once on, we had to get back off again, maintaining a steady evenness on the platform. We were not allowed to talk once the activity began.

Billy challenged us further by casually mentioning that no group had completed the task of getting on the raft in fewer than thirty minutes. He gave us ten minutes to form a plan.

I knew exactly what to do. I'd grown up on boats, after all. As a kid, my commodity at sea was my size. I was small enough to stay out of the way but also heavy enough to help keep a fast-moving sailboat from tipping. I'd often played the part of a glorified sandbag. By eight, I'd learned to feel the keel of the boat beneath me and move my body to rebalance accordingly. I spent a few summers enjoying the attention of being the most coveted child crew member, though nobody bothered to ask if I liked sailing. I'm not sure I even considered it myself.

Our balancing task was much the same as keeping a sailboat on an even keel, but ten minutes was barely enough to explain a lifetime of nuance to the crew in front of me.

"Do you trust me?" I asked the group. I was exhilarated and could already feel the win. A quietly competitive people pleaser, I thrilled at the idea of impressing Billy and my teammates. They did trust me and said so without hesitation. I realized I felt a part of myself waking up at the challenge. I liked it.

I was first to step on the "raft," and I chose my teammate Hope next by pointing at her. Tall and strong, Hope moved to the middle of the raft to act as the ballast around which we would all move.

Hope stood with her legs wide on the platform in an inverted V, straddling the unseen roller beneath the raft. Slowly, I pointed to members of the group, adding people while simultaneously placing myself in the position of counterweight. I matched every step as my teammates slowly slid in place, using my feet to feel where they and I needed to be. Once a member was settled, they could relax and encourage the others. My attunement was fierce. It was the same skill I applied to being a therapist.

Our team included my pro-athlete friend as well as a woman the size of a pixie, which made the physics complicated but not impossible. The going was slow and exacting. Every time a new member moved an inch on the raft, I counter-moved. My legs wobbled, my feet ached, and sweat clung to my forehead and dripped down my back.

In just over eighteen minutes, everyone was standing perfectly balanced on the raft.

Billy whooped, clapped his hands, and laughed out loud. He took one minute to compliment our hard work before telling us it was even harder to get down. He wasn't wrong in that the raft bounced slightly as each person stepped off. After a near miss with the first departure, I learned to ground my weight in a crouch each time a foot came off the boards. Halfway through our descent, Hope waved her arms in distress, pointing at her legs, which had begun to cramp, so the athlete subbed in. Thighs and glutes for days, he delighted in playing the relief pitcher to save our win.

As expected, we also killed the second half of the task, finishing again in record time, according to Billy. The group laughed and high-fived.

Billy led us through a quick debrief before we moved on to the next task on the course that was deeper in the woods. I stood beaming as my teammates cited my leadership qualities, quick thinking, and hardworking calm.

"It was like we didn't even need to be here," one of the early raft steppers said. "I was so relaxed, I meditated."

Hope smiled. "I liked getting to help. I felt like I mattered. I didn't like being replaced." I smiled and gave her a wink.

"I was sort of hoping to sub in for Meghan." I turned to face the voice of the young man, still a teen really, around whom I generally felt awkward and old. He spoke to Billy, avoiding my eyes, and I felt surprised by a quick snap of shame. "I understood what she was doing, and it looked hard. I like hard. She's a badass, but I would have liked to have helped more." I heard his words and felt the quiet pulse of a familiar worry. He wasn't happy, which might have meant I wasn't safe.

But I'd won all the blue ribbons of field day, and it was my shining moment.

As we walked down the hill to the next activity, Billy fell in step.

"Who's your therapist?" he asked lightly.

"Jo," I replied. I assumed he planned to report on my triumph.

"And you're working on codependency, I assume?"

I felt the thud in my stomach as solidly as if he'd actually punched me. Panic surged, and I sucked in for breath.

My therapist mind held a working definition of codependency at the ready: the act of being so invested in another person's happiness or emotional well-being that you lack the ability to function independently or to identify and meet your own needs.

Billy's voice was soft but firm.

"Seems to me I just watched one woman carry ten others on her back."

I suddenly felt dizzy and sank into the tall grass.

The truth of my behavior washed over me, and my entire emotional destruction began to make brutal sense.

After the loss of my parents, I didn't know how to belong to myself. Despite my previous years of therapeutic work and my clinical training, I had never really stopped belonging to my mother and my father. I still lived by most of their rules and their beliefs—women were helpers who minimized needs in order to be loved. Without them to please or impress, I was a boat unmoored.

Kneeling in the grass, I wept for the lifetime of relationships I'd created based on offering to others—some way to help, hoping to be thought of or considered in return.

I'd built a life with Mike that was different from the one I'd come from but not different enough. He didn't need me to help him or put him first—there was plenty of room for my needs, but *I* denied them. I gave things to our marriage and family that I needed and wanted in the hopes he would give them back. I insisted on living by the rule that minimizing myself was the best way to stay safe and be loved. I "helped" when no one asked me to, which might not have actually been helping at all.

Sitting in the hot sun in the sticky hay-like grass, I felt my internal curtain drop. Once the truth of me was exposed it was impossible to unsee.

"Oh my God. I did this to myself," I gasped. "I'm still doing it."

Billy knelt next to me and rubbed my back.

"You are okay," he said over and over.

And when I finished crying, he did not help me up.

"A codependent relapse," Jo called it later as we sat on the ranch house's porch in the fading evening light. We watched a pair of cardinals hop along the fence rail. "You fell back into patterns from childhood that had been your best efforts at feeling safe and protected." Jo's voice was warm and understanding.

"I can't believe how much of my life has always been about staying in the lines, looking for approval, and needing people to like me." A minute later, I said, "I keep thinking how I never would have come here if my mother was alive."

Jo raised an eyebrow as if to say "Duh."

"Even for a different reason, even if I really needed it, I doubt I would have come."

"Why?" Jo seemed interested.

"Because the kind of woman who checks herself into an expensive inpatient facility is not the kind of woman my mother would have liked." The words rushed out quickly.

"How do you know?" Jo asked.

"Trust me, Jo. I know."

"So you would have stayed sick rather than disappoint or displease her?"

I was silent. I wasn't sure I knew the answer.

Suddenly I thought of my mother rocking gently in our kitchen in the chair my father had made. I saw her closed eyes and little me sitting at her feet, rubbing thin, inexpensive drug-store hand lotion into her tired heels.

Jo casually pulled out a small glass tube with a roller-top like a lip gloss. I recognized it as one of the essential oils from the gift shop and watched as she rubbed the liquid on her wrists, upper lip, and behind her ears. Her constant care of herself felt inspirational.

"So, what would happen if you stopped helping others?"

Our conversation was relaxed but still therapy.

"I would never get to need anything. I wouldn't deserve anything, and people would resent me."

"*Who* would resent you?" Jo kept her voice neutral and curious.

"Everyone."

My memory offered quick snippets: childhood car trips where my need to use the bathroom garnered a collective groan. The hours I spent helping my mother in the kitchen in the hopes that she would see me as important and lovable.

I saw myself in my midtwenties, my mother cornering me in her kitchen before bed. As she hugged me, she said in her sweet and sleepy way, "You were the one that never really needed me." She meant it as a compliment, but even in the moment the truth of her words took my breath away.

"Why *resent* you?" Jo's question brought me back to the present.

"For needing them."

Jo reached over and put her hand on top of my hand before she said, "Well, no wonder you got so lost. Very few people can find the next right way without some kind of help."

I nodded slowly, taking in her words with a deep breath.

"So, can you let it go now?"

I stopped rocking. Jo stopped too. She looked me in the face. "Can you let go of the idea that you are only worthy of love once you have given something first?"

I pictured Mike with his easy smile on the day we signed our first mortgage. My insides had melted with panic and fear, but his hug was warm and his words soothing. "We're fine," he said in a soft, confident tone I completely trusted. I remembered our three kids sitting at our messy kitchen counter dissolving into giggles over something meaningless.

Mike and our kids didn't see me as broken; they saw me as unwell. If I needed to do less to find my new way forward, it would be fine. *It would not be a problem. It would just be different.*

"Can you just accept yourself as *enough*?" Jo emphasized the word with her southern drawl.

I cracked a small, sly smile. I pulled down the bracelet on my right arm and flashed Jo my tattoo. For the past three years I'd had the word *enough* permanently inked in steady, black cursive on the inside of my wrist.

THIRTY-FIVE

I was grateful to begin to feel a yearning to be near my family and home again. As my three weeks in treatment wound down, I thought of Mike and the kids more often. Little things—a glimpse of a game of football on TV that I knew Daniel and Mike would also be watching together; a board game I'd been roped into playing after dinner that I knew the kids would love. I began to feel a growing need to hold my children and know the minutiae of their days. I missed Mike's voice, his smile, and what it felt like to stand near him.

A few days before my discharge date, I felt a specific sort of tension softening. I could finally trust my body not to weaponize my grief against me. Like a spring thaw, the pictures of death had largely melted away, and in their place, I found occasional rest, laughter, and ample gratitude.

At Dr. G.'s suggestion, I booked a meeting with an integrative practitioner whose office was an hour off campus. Everyone hoped the sleep specialist might help me find more reliable rest, as I still struggled with sleeping through the night.

As with everything in treatment, the travel to the doctor was therapeutic. I talked my way into the Yukon's passenger seat next to my driver, Alan. I was struck by how much sitting next to him reminded me of running errands with my father as a kid. Both men drove confidently, humming along to music and asking an occasional question. I felt a young sort of vulnerable that reminded me of a feeling of safety I craved but hadn't had in years.

I'd become more introverted during my time at Foundations. I was learning to sit with my anxiety to be liked by practicing stillness and quiet. Alan offered me easy conversation instead. He reported on the history and context of the landscape as we drove past, happy to answer questions as to how he'd become a driver for the facility and what it was like to live your whole life in Tennessee.

"Well, we've traveled, but I can't say we'd ever think of moving," Alan replied.

"It's the cowboy boots and the cooking, right? Can't leave the catfish," I joked.

Alan laughed lightly. "Well, that, and our son's buried here."

Alan's answer was simple and crushing. His son, Glen, had died of an overdose five years earlier. Glen had become addicted to various substances as a teen. Sober for almost twenty years, he shattered his leg in a motorcycle accident. After surgery, he'd been given painkillers. Alan and his wife, Cheryl, hadn't even known.

A friend told a heartbroken Cheryl about Foundations's

grief and loss workshop. She credited it with saving her life. Eventually, Alan went as well. Their therapist suggested acts of service to honor their son. Alan liked to drive. A year after Glen's death, Alan brought his first client from the airport to treatment, the way he wished he could have done for his son.

"It's a delicate job," Alan explained. "People are often pretty sick when they get here, really scared, you know?"

I smiled. Of course I knew. Though Alan hadn't been the one to drive me from the aiport, I remembered shaking so much during the ride, my driver had resorted to turning on the heat in the SUV. At one point, she pulled the car over to make a call, which now occurred to me was likely to the treatment team to let them know what state they should expect me to be in when we walked through the door. Remembering made me feel grateful for the progress I'd made.

Alan waited for me during my appointment. It was a more comprehensive "under the hood" checkup than a normal primary-care appointment and generated a list of supple-ments to hopefully balance out the hormonal shifts that may have been causing the 3:00 a.m. wake-ups.

When I walked out into the Tennessee sunshine, I found Alan leaning against the hood of the SUV, holding a cup of coffee, with his head tilted up, eyes closed facing the sun.

"All done," I announced cheerfully. I was looking forward to the drive back with my new friend, another indicator that my trauma had thawed considerably.

"How about we take the scenic route?" Alan asked. "We've got lots of fancy houses out this way."

Alan was an impressive guide. He pointed out large gates and groves protecting the ranch homes of a wide variety of celebrities from music and film. For a minute I imagined I was a tourist and not a client from a mental health center.

Alan drove me through Franklin, which he described as a quaint town with rising real estate prices and tourist cafés with five-dollar cups of coffee.

What I saw of the place from the blacked-out window of the SUV reminded me of the town where I lived with Mike and the kids: shops selling earth-colored linen, moderately priced jewelry, and high-end baseball caps.

Alan made a hard right turn, and I noticed a sharp flick of tension in my chest. A quick twist of nausea hit my stomach, and I felt my jaw clench. I grabbed the door handle in the hope of riding out the sensation, but suddenly I was gripping and flailing. We made it one more block before my eyes blurred dark and my lungs began to collapse.

"Hey, you okay?" Alan's voice was alert and almost tense.

"No!" I sucked in the small amount of air I could pull into my lungs. Alan turned his head to my panicked face and, in a move that reminded me of my husband, carefully pulled the car over onto a grassy shoulder. I yanked my door handle and tumbled from the too-high seat onto the earth. Kneeling on all fours, I worked hard to steady my breath and stay conscious.

Alan remained calm. He approached me carefully, show-ing me both his palms like a magician before he placed one steadily on my back. He ran his knuckle gently down my back-bone and up again.

"You're okay. Deep breaths. You're doin' great." I felt comforted by the deepening in his twang.

I'd heard the general comparisons between heart attacks and panic attacks—both sent signals to the body through an incredible surge of adrenaline. I'd taken a training from a clinician who worked in an ER after 9/11 and had spent days teaching petrified New Yorkers the difference between the symptoms. Hot and dizzy on the inside, I knew it was my head that was on fire, not my heart. This panic attack wasn't quite to the level of driving home from the Cape, but it wasn't far off.

I rubbed my tears across my cheeks, wondering how I'd gone from congratulating myself on my progress to nearly vomiting on the side of the road. I knew recovery wasn't linear, but it was hard not to take this episode as a setback. I suddenly felt less convinced that leaving in a few days would be a good idea.

Alan stayed with me. His voice and movements projected calm and safety. Soon I was able to match my breath to the cadence of his words. My throat felt raw, and small patches on my face burned as though it had been singed. Wordlessly, Alan helped me to my feet, opened the car door, and steadied me as I stepped up and in.

"This happens," he said kindly.

Alan got in on the driver's side and checked his mirrors, then we were moving again. Within seconds, my adrenaline bottomed out, and I fell into an exhausted sleep. My head leaned precariously against the passenger-side window.

A gentle knock roused me from my nap. Laura, the aftercare coordinator, poked her head through the window of the SUV, where Alan had politely left me resting. She gave me a 30 percent smile.

"I heard the ride home was something."

"It was. I'm not sure why."

"Panic attack?"

"Oh, for sure."

"Any ideas?"

"One second Franklin is reminding me of home, the next second I'm in the grass."

"Hmm." Laura was thoughtful. "How many days until you leave?"

"Three."

"Huh. Okay. I'll check in with the team."

I nodded, but my eyelids insisted on closing again. I was completely depleted and not ready to face whatever my panic might mean about going home. It wasn't uncommon for clients to extend their stay to maximize treatment benefits, but it hadn't yet been suggested to me, and I could in no way afford it.

Laura circled back at dinner. I fully expected her to suggest a clinical retreat complete with a recommendation to double down on sessions with Jo.

I was holding a tray loaded with lasagna and a huge green salad when I saw her sidling up.

"What's your schedule look like tomorrow?" She had a beautiful smile, but at that moment I wasn't sure I could trust it.

"I have an individual session and then equine therapy. Why?"

"Well, we want to get you back on the horse." Laura chuckled at her joke and followed me to a table, where she explained the plan.

In the two hours since I'd returned, the team (every practitioner who worked with me) had convened and come to the consensus that I should go back to Franklin. I'd expected a cautious response, but my team projected confidence.

"It's not uncommon for people to decompensate a little before discharge," Laura explained. "The last thing we want is for you to worry that you can't function outside of here." That was, of course, my exact fear. "Today you felt terrified, but there was no actual threat. That feeling might happen again, and it's your job to know how to get help."

I felt my head spin slightly. I'd coached my own clients in the same way. *"You are not a failure because you need support—just human."* I heard Jo's voice in my head. Could anyone actually help me? Why would they want to? Where was the line of what was too much to ask? My eyes pricked with tears as I voiced my fears to Laura.

"What if I can't figure out what to ask for?" There was a slight tremor in my voice.

"Your job isn't to figure out how to need the least amount possible, remember?"

I nodded. This truth was the cornerstone of my treatment. "It's also not your job to figure out how much help is available or who will give it to you. 'Help' is a complete sentence."

Laura said she planned to bring me back to Franklin in the morning. She would find a bench to sit on and, like a mom keeping her eye on a child at a playground, she'd just be there if I needed her. Laura relayed my team's confidence that I was ready to be out in the world, with the understanding that it was okay to need some practice.

"Besides," Laura graciously insisted, "I have a book I'm dying to finish. It will practically be a day off for me." Her kindness made me weep a little. Just as I imagine the team hoped, I began to believe I really was ready to take on the very thing that hours earlier had brought me to my knees: going home.

The next day, I was back in Franklin with Laura installed on a bench reading what turned out to be an abnormal-psychology textbook. Given her generosity, I decided to let it slide. I stood hovering, at a loss for where to start.

"Just try something that feels possible," Laura encouraged.

I decided I could walk up the street past the little shops, maybe go into one or two. It was 10:00 a.m. I could get a coffee. I used to drink coffee before my sleep got wonky. I saw a mostly full café with a long line that I took as a good sign. I would get in line and order a latte.

The sounds and smells, colors and movements of the café were borderline overstimulating, but I felt encouraged that with a few deep breaths I could loosen the tension in my chest. A friendly teenage clerk waited on the man in front of me. The two laughed easily and almost too loud over local high school sports. Suddenly it was my turn.

I had been rehearsing my words. "I'll have a latte with skim milk, please."

The young man's face crinkled with kindness. "This is the pie line."

"Pie line?"

My head rushed and my arms flooded cold. I tried not to give in to the panic, but I could feel my mind begin to get cloudy.

"Don't worry." The young man's voice was warm and encouraging. "Pie is good. I can also get you a coffee, but you've already waited in line for pie."

"I don't like pie." It seemed true when I said it. Was it? I felt suddenly self-conscious and unsure.

"Impossible. Who doesn't like pie?" He said it loud enough for folks behind me in line to chuckle. I shrugged, speechless. "Well, do you know *anyone* who likes pie? Because this lemon meringue is award-winning. In fact, there's a busload of seniors on their way here just on account of this pie."

I felt sure I'd seen pie in the treatment center. Had people eaten it? Was it good? Not good?

"I think I have friends who like pie."

The clerk's smile widened, flashing his white teeth.

"Excellent. Should we get them a pie, then?"

I felt my body regulate and my thoughts come back online. This was what my treatment team wanted. I would get jacked up, of course, but it was more important for me to know that I could recover—even if it meant asking for help.

"Well, I actually have twenty-two friends, and there's a bunch of staff. I'll need more than one pie." I wondered for a second if buying pie would seem too much like doing for others, but eventually dismissed it. Everyone back at the program knew about my "field trip," and I hoped the pie would be a good way to celebrate my success.

The friendly clerk's name was Jayson, and he was delighted for both of us.

"I can't imagine getting to try chess pie for the first time again!" Jayson shook his head with his broad smile when I confirmed that I'd never had it. My pie enthusiast did some quick math and suggested I buy at least five, making me promise I would try a bite of each one. I laughed as Jayson playfully blew goodbye kisses to the desserts as he packed them up—fruit, chocolate, and pudding pies with top crust or lattice work, and some with whipped cream.

"These pies are so good they are going to ruin you for pies forever!" Jayson said as he wrote the names on the outside of the boxes in large methodical block lettering.

What had started as an awkward scenario melted into a warm and easy interaction. The ghost of my old self seemed to peek her head around the corner. I was grateful for Jayson's youth, enthusiasm, and concrete help.

When I finished paying, I still had an hour of life practice to do. I'd come in for a coffee and ended up with an armful of dessert. Jayson offered to put the pies in the walk-in cooler so I could come back for them later, and I immediately accepted. He held the door for me, and when I said, "I'll be back in an hour," I was suddenly hit by a rogue wave of fear.

"Actually, can I ask you a question? Will you help me?" My eyes searched Jayson's face.

"Sure." His answer was instant. I was grateful to have been given my cell phone in case of an emergency.

"Do you think you could text me in an hour to remind me to pick up my pies?" After my mother died, I'd become so easily distracted, I threw my American Express card away six times. I knew forgetting the pies was a real possibility.

Jayson did not laugh at me or tell me to set an alert on my phone. He did not shift his weight awkwardly from foot to foot, keeping his eyes down. He didn't wonder out loud what kind of weirdo needed a pie reminder. Instead, he smiled and said, "Sure," then entered my phone number into his. He pinged me exactly an hour later.

"It's your pies. Don't forget us!"

A soft warmth rose in my chest when I saw his text, offering me the safety net I needed. Without judgment. And without expecting anything in exchange.

When I got back to the bench, Laura wasn't there, so I sat down to wait. Looking down at the pies stacked neatly and drawn up with red-and-white string, I found a sudden catch in my throat. Jayson was just the last in an incredibly long list of people who had made making my way back to my life filled with my loved ones possible. I bowed my head as in prayer and whispered their names out loud to myself. I started with the outer orbits—all the people at Foundations—and moved inward. Friends like family; my siblings and their partners; and finally, my father and then my mother. When Laura found me a few minutes later, my eyes were red, but my body was buzzing with gratitude.

Jo told me later that bringing pie back to all the other "kids in treatment" was a very mom sort of thing to do. She suggested that maybe I'd been practicing asking for what I wanted and needed the way children typically do while also still playing the part of the adult who would make sure those needs were met.

With only two days left at Foundations, I understood that trauma from my childhood combined with my parents' deaths were only some of the bricks from the path of my undoing; I had laid others myself. I had more work to do, and I felt well enough to believe I could do it.

THIRTY-SIX

The seasons turned almost overnight as the southern heat overcorrected into mornings of frost and fog. It was time to go home.

As one would expect, the goodbyes in treatment were not wasted. On my second day I had been present for the center's send-off of a young woman named Ally. Just nineteen, she had lived in treatment for nearly a year; even the kitchen staff joined in celebrating her last day. I didn't know her story, but I could feel her transformation.

Very few inpatient departures are ever a straight-up success story. For my clients, Foundations was often part of a constellation of treatments. It was helpful to remember that every single one of them had told me they felt scared leaving.

My "graduation" seemed to take several of my friends by surprise, likely because I didn't need the didactic teaching, so my stay was a week shorter than most. I sat on the hearth of the same fireplace that had greeted me on my first day and felt a familiar sense of sadness. My spot in treatment would be easily filled by a new client arriving in the next few days. The people I left behind would make friends with my replacement, and my name would become just one on the list of the center's never-ending rotation of trauma clients. It struck me that the leaving ceremony created an existential paradox: on the one hand reminding you that you mattered, while on the other reminding you that you were utterly replaceable. After a childhood spent craving and fearing the cost of attention, the message that we all mattered, yet none of us were permanent, felt like a raw kind of truth.

"In some ways, all of life is just a series of comings and goings," Jo said when she hugged me at the end of our last session.

Before my exit meeting began, one of the CAs stuck his head out of the main office and waved in my direction. With my brow furrowed in confusion, I followed him back to his desk, where he held up a piece of mail with my name on it. I waited as he cut open and searched the yellow-orange envelope. I didn't immediately recognize the handwriting. I had been more relieved than disappointed when I hadn't received daily "love and miss you" letters from my kids over the last three weeks. This envelope's shape promised something other than a child's drawing. I took the already opened mailer and tilted it so the item slipped out into my hand.

It was a high-end lip gloss in the perfect shade of coral.

The card was from Stacy and said only "Miss you." Still miles away from being back to a life that included makeup, I could hear the whispers of my world in D.C. I was grateful we were returning to each other.

I made my way back to the fireplace, where everyone had finally gathered, clutching my lip gloss like an amulet. Fear and fragility twinged ever so slightly in my lower back, but I sat at the head of the class, feeling both exposed and excited with all eyes on me.

Jo started us off by handing me small gifts she'd picked out personally: a journal "to get me writing" and a pair of mismatched socks in sweet reference to the hospital story from before my mom died. Both gifts made me tear up, not for their value but also absolutely for their value.

What unfolded next, I'd seen and been a part of before. Jo pulled out a heavy, coin-shaped keychain with the name of the center emblazoned across the top. As was the ritual, Jo pressed the key chain into her palm and closed her fingers around it. "Your life is an extraordinary gift. May you live according to your own compass and inspire others with the goodness of what you find and create." Her eyes twinkled. "As your parting gift, I press in 'self' that never leaves you."

The key chain slowly passed from staff to client, each person offering advice, well wishes, or telling a story. Some were touching and some were poignant. "I remember the first time I heard you sing in the hallway," one of my group members said, flipping the key chain through her fingers, "and I thought, she'll find her voice her own way."

In his wizard-like manner, Billy complimented me on my

hard work and my courage. "You surprised me," he said in a slow drawl. "I never thought I'd get you on that zip line." The group burst into laughter at the memory of me screaming as I tore across canopy heights. "I hope you continue to take risks." Billy smiled and winked at me as he passed the key chain.

When the coin landed in the palm of the oldest member of the group, he said, "I hope you know you're a great mom." His words were unexpected, and I put my head in my hands to hide. Undaunted by my show of emotion, he continued. "I was in this room that first night when you called your kids." He motioned to the back, where the landlines sat idle next to the oversized armchairs. "How was your day, buddy? Tell me everything." He mimicked my voice perfectly. Hearty laughter and nodding, smiling heads bounced around the room.

"Any feelings I need to know about?" I heard my own phrase echo in a woman's voice diagonally across from me. I looked into her heavy, mirthful eyes. I knew her less than I did some of the others. "I always tried to be in here when you called your kids." She looked away when she said it. "Not eavesdropping or anything. I just loved imagining what it would be like to have been asked that when I was a kid." I nodded a thank-you, and my words caught in my throat. "I think being a good mom is a tribute to your mom, even if she died," she added bluntly.

I teared up again, and Jo rubbed my leg.

"How many of you intentionally listened to Meghan with her family?" Jo asked. "Hands up. No one is in trouble." At least half of the hands raised; many were my motherless peers.

"Thank you," I said in earnest. I took a deep breath and made eye contact with each listener. For the first time, I felt the possibility of my mother's legacy expand past being dead. I began to understand that we never stop needing our parents and that we can be parented in ways we don't expect even after they die.

In previous ceremonies, departing clients had gifted totems to those who continued in treatment. The gifts felt like a way to keep connected to the web of support. I loved the idea. In the first ceremony I attended, a woman I'd met for only a matter of minutes wrapped a thin cuff bracelet on my arm with the words "You are a warrior" inscribed inside.

"Wear it until you know it's time to give it away," she said to each of us.

I was still wearing the bracelet when I shopped for my own goodbye gifts. I clicked purchase on a cart of small black anchors tethered to lengths of leather that could be worn as either a necklace or a bracelet.

"I love the concept they teach us here to use our breath as an anchor," I explained to the group. "I used to think that my mother was my anchor, the weight that kept me safe, but I've discovered it's me. That's the way it has to be because"—I paused and took a breath, a little afraid of the truth I needed to hear myself speak—"I need me the most."

Heads nodded again as everyone, clients and staff, took a leather string from the basket and passed it. Staring out at my group of co-healers, I understood that not everyone would walk back to a life that had waited for them. Not everyone would get well here. Not everyone would even survive their trauma in the end.

"Thank you." I nodded to the group. With my lower back aching in earnest, I stood and gave final hugs. Holding fear in one hand and hope in the other, I walked across the threshold I'd first crossed just three short weeks ago.

THIRTY-SEVEN

Diana, again my driver, stood to collect me from the same steps where she'd left me dazed and shaking. Her smile was so warm, I hardly recognized her.

"Look at you!" she said with excitement in her voice. I was genuinely surprised by how much Diana seemed to have changed. After I climbed back into her SUV and carefully arranged myself without straining my back, I suddenly realized that of the two of us, it was likely me, not Diana, who was different. As the car pulled out of the driveway and the ranch disappeared behind us, small bursts of energy exploded inside me. I wasn't sure if they were from excitement or fear or, probably, both.

The airport was blurry and loud. I played soothing cello music through my headphones and put on sunglasses, but by the time I made it to the gate, I was sweating. The waiting area was almost full, so I settled myself mostly uncomfortably in an empty seat in an adjacent gate from which a plane had just departed.

I waited to board until the flight attendant announced: "Last call for Southwest flight 167 to Reagan National Airport." I'd underestimated the slow pace my aching back required, and soon I heard my name called over the loudspeaker: "Passenger Meghan Jarvis, please report to gate D6. Your flight is leaving."

I forced myself to move more quickly. It turned out I really did want to go home.

I slept the whole flight. When I hit the terminal in D.C., I kept my eyes on my feet as I made my way outside and into a cab. Mike and I had agreed that an airport reunion would be too much for everyone.

As the familiar D.C. landmarks passed outside the window, I felt something inside me settle. I found myself aching to hear Maia's voice, and I called her for the first time in a month.

"Hell-oooo." I could hear love and trepidation in her voice.

"I'm on my way home." I sounded surer than I felt. "And I'm okay." I heard Maia give a literal sigh of relief. "I can't talk yet, but I will."

"Whatever you need." She'd been offering the same thing since I was eleven. Whatever I needed. Was this the first time I truly heard it?

"Love you," I said, with a catch in my voice. It was a crying kind of day.

"Love you," she replied, and I knew it was true.

• • •

When the taxi dropped me at my own front porch, I stood for a moment peering unnoticed through the glass into the kitchen. I could see my kids laughing and playing an energetic card game with the smiley sitter I'd hired just before I left. I knew from my few calls with the kids that the sitter had become a safe after-school landing pad in my absence. She seemed as comfortable in my home as I now felt out of place.

I cracked the front door and was relieved by the immediate thunder of feet and rush of hugs. The lights of the kitchen felt overly bright and the music far too loud. I tried not to wince in the noise and the movement and chaos of our reunion. The kids settled back to their game with the sitter, which left me without a seat. Self-conscious and excluded, I lugged my bag upstairs myself. Mike and I had agreed to keep the day as normal as possible for the kids, so he was still at work.

Part of me was grateful to be reminded that I was not the sole focus of our children's lives and that my leaving had not devastated them. I'm not sure what kind of homecoming I expected, but I felt childish for wanting a bit more fuss—a *Welcome Home* sign, maybe some tears? I sat on the chaise at the foot of our bed and pulled out the small gifts I'd somehow thought to buy the kids during one weekend outing to Target. For a few seconds I let myself pretend I had just been on an extended business trip.

When my eyes fell again on the open suitcase, I noted the shapeless, drab clothes worn week after week in treatment spilling out the sides. I heaved myself to standing and walked to the utility closet in the hallway, where, underneath a multipack of hand soap and a half-full carton of recessed flood light bulbs, I found a trash bag. I stalked back to the suitcase and scooped up everything but my hiking boots with the dirt of Tennessee stuck in their treads. I never wanted to see those clothes again.

I'd intended to drag the bag toward the trash can at the far corner of the room but made it only as far as my bed. I flopped myself down on Mike's side and inhaled the scent of his pillow that was flecked with a few stray hairs. I picked up the giant history tome from his bedside table. A crinkled photo of us with the kids at his parents' fiftieth anniversary party in England—a convenient bookmark—peeked out the top. With my hand still wrapped around the red drawstring of the plastic bag, I pulled it without thinking into the bed and hugged it to me. Within minutes I was asleep.

I woke in darkness with Mike still dressed in his suit, shoes still on, spooned into the space around me, covering me like a shield. I lay for an hour, basking in the feeling of safety and love before drifting off again.

I wasn't fully healed. But I was home.

THIRTY-EIGHT

My ear surgery was scheduled for the week I returned home.

I hadn't given much thought to the small bones that were apparently still growing across my ear canal, and I tried to resist fear and worry at my pre-op appointment. My doctor quickly explained that during the three-hour procedure he would cut off my ear entirely, then use a drill to file down the small bones growing like stalactites and stalagmites across my ear canal. The bulk of our meeting focused more on insurance and payment than it did on providing any expectation of post-op healing. I imagine as a therapist, if a client of mine recovering from PTSD was scheduled for a surgery so early in her emotional healing, I might have suggested postponing.

Mike and I arrived at the local teaching hospital in the early morning when it was still dark out. The waiting room already felt like a crowded bus station. The older adults were attended to by caretakers, while small children wiggled in parents' laps. All of our bodies were in various stages of brokenness, waiting for the chance to be further injured in the hopes of ultimately healing.

Mike and I were brought to a hallway cordoned off into a small room by familiar thin cotton curtains. The fluorescent lights, the acrid smell of ammonia, and intermittent beeping sounds were agitating. It took me a few minutes to realize my body had time-traveled to the place where I was waiting with my father for the results of a test or treatment. This time it was me on the gurney, and Mike was the one holding his breath.

I changed into the overly laundered hospital gown and lay down on the bed. There wasn't a chair for Mike, and we hadn't thought to bring a bag for the clothes I'd come in. The doctor entered as Mike was stuffing my bra awkwardly into the computer bag he'd brought in the hopes of getting some work done. I hadn't decided if I thought he was being practical or ridiculous.

After a few minutes the surgeon left with a brusque "See you in there." Mike leaned in to kiss my forehead. I found myself weeping, struggling to recall if I'd kissed my mother similarly when the sweet nurse with the heavy Boston accent wheeled her, terrified, toward the ultrasound room when I'd taken her to the hospital. As a tech lifted the sedation mask to my face and asked me to count backward from twenty, I remembered with relief that I had.

When I woke up, I was somehow sitting in a chair, my hair matted with blood and a large bandage attached to my ear. My head was fuzzy and my vision delayed. I couldn't hear much of anything, but my van Gogh jokes were at the ready.

When I asked for Mike, the nurse told me, "I paged him, and I went out to the waiting area, but he must have left."

I felt generally confused but not at the absurdity of her statement. Mike had been holding the anxiety for both of us. There was zero possibility he'd left.

Maybe it was the painkillers, maybe it was my rising fear, or maybe my righteous anger was finding its way back to me, but I just started yelling his name.

"MIKE! MIKE JARVIS." Within seconds, he was at my side, insisting he hadn't been called.

The surgeon declared he was happy with the "lines," whatever that meant, and deemed us—me unable to see, walk, or hear—fine to go home.

"You've got to be fucking kidding me," I said, incredulous, as Mike left me in the wheelchair at the hospital entrance and ran to find the valet. The parking garage was riddled with construction, cars honking chaotically, and beeping emergency vehicles. My head ached in blinding pain. The remnants of the anesthesia had left my body weak, and I could barely help Mike get me into the passenger seat.

My recovery turned out to be much more complicated and painful than anyone anticipated. I spent the first two days completely sedated and the next few in and out of consciousness. On the fifth day, I woke to pain so intense it made my skull feel like a balloon made of glass. My head rang on the inside whenever I moved. It took a full day to unwind the problem, but apparently a mistyped prescription label meant I had spent nearly a week underdosed with pain medication.

The swelling I had been told to expect to go down in seven days took more than a month, and vertigo kept me from driving. I had essentially no hearing in my left ear, while my right ear overworked to modulate noises that sounded too close or too loud.

My sensory world was exhausting. The easiest place to be was asleep in my bed. If there was any bright side to all this, it was that I was too sick and exhausted to feel much of my grief. Like a Venn diagram, my physical and emotional pain had overlapping symptoms. I was exhausted and irritable, and my concentration was nonexistent. I knew logically my body was healing, but it was hard not to feel pathetic and broken.

My hearing loss was particularly scary.

"How important is listening in your line of work?" the audiologist asked without irony a month after my surgery. I had failed almost every marker. I laughed so hard I pulled the headphones out of the wall. It was early December, and I had already been out of work for five months. I was scheduled to return to the office the following month, but at the rate I was recovering, I might miss the promised window.

It's a bit much, don't you think? I texted Maia later.

The writers are definitely hitting us over the head with the whole traumatized trauma therapist plot, she replied.

Then, one day in mid-December, I sat on the couch (again) as my son played a video game. He asked out of habit, "Should I turn off the sound?" The obnoxious music and overly loud soundtrack was generally hard for me on a good hearing day. I paused and listened. Like the quiet just after breaking glass, everything sounded normal and inoffensive. For the first time in as long as I could remember, I sat in my living room with my children and my husband nearby, in no pain or discomfort. Instead, my head exploded with confetti of gratitude.

Stacy and Maribeth's long-ago suggestion that I try to make it back to the office by January now seemed prescient. I'd left work in late July for my vacation with my mother. I took August off for her death and September for my illness. October and November were spent in various stages of trauma treatment. I'd lost December to the pain, tears, and dizziness that no one had expected. My body and mind seemed to be finally healing. I hoped I was finally learning to carry my grief rather than buckle under the weight of it.

THIRTY-NINE

Before I attempted to set a foot back in my office, I sat down again for a supervision lunch with Maribeth and Stacy. I was grateful neither had over- or underseasoned me with check-ins since I'd left for treatment. I was excited to see them again in person.

Stacy seemed to sense I was anxious to talk through what being in treatment meant to my clinical work.

"Have you decided how to explain your absence to your clients?" she asked.

We had each been trained that time and space in a therapy session belongs solely to the client—the job of a therapist is to keep her story out of the room. Sure, there had been maternity leaves, short absences due to illness, and emergencies that brought up complicated feelings for clients—examples that fell well inside the lines of typical experience. But none of us had been trained on how to address the *therapist's* mental health crisis.

Maribeth was more circumspect. "What will it take to get *you* back in the therapist's chair?" she asked. "What do *you* need to take back your role in the room?"

My reply was simple: "I need to tell the truth."

This time I knew my own answer. It would mean stretching boundaries that other therapists described as inflexible. I did not ask permission.

My friends both nodded.

I quickly ran through my client list and considered the impact sharing my own trauma experience might have on each person. I was delighted that my memory afforded me perfect recall of my roster.

"I'll give a quick summary of my PTSD and treatment and ask if they have questions," I said, thinking out loud. "I have at least three people who have lost moms. It might be triggering for them."

"It's *already* been triggering for them," Maribeth reminded me. "It will be better with an invitation to talk about it."

At the end of the hour, my effort to get back to the office felt as though it was shared across a team. It seemed like obvious, measurable progress that I was able to consider other people's mental health for a change.

The morning I went back to the office, I spent an hour changing my outfit. Most of my old clothes felt odd and ill-fitting. My uniform had been a casual dress paired with a high heel, but those clothes now felt like a cover story of "put-togetherness" that had long since been blown. I settled on a slightly more fashionable version of the leggings and oversized sweater I had been wearing for months. My outfit felt less professional but more honest.

At Stacy and Maribeth's suggestion I planned to ease myself back into the chair. I'd start off with only a couple of clients a day instead of my usual five to seven.

On the first Tuesday in January, four months and twenty-five days after my mother's death (two months and eight days since returning from treatment), I walked back into my office. The morning hadn't gone smoothly; I couldn't even find my office keys. I'd looked in my purse, coat pockets, and the kitchen junk drawer before finally remembering that I'd put them on the key chain Foundations had gifted me. I had stored them with my precious things in my jewelry box when I came back from treatment.

Mike walked with me, like a parent taking a child to their first day of preschool. We rode up in the elevator in silence. At the threshold of my small suite, I told him I wanted to go in alone. I stepped into the pale-blue room accented with soft gray carpet and carefully selected midcentury modern furniture. My office looked just as I remembered—my coffee cups, my magazines, my small tray of business cards with my name and phone number printed over the whimsical outline of a couch were all exactly as I'd left them. As I scanned the room, my eyes landed on the shriveled remnants of the jade plant I'd been given by a high school student more than a decade ago. I solemnly placed the dead dry plant carcass into the trash. Life and death always, everywhere.

After a few minutes of reorientation, I finally sat myself down in my pale-blue therapist's chair. Everything felt familiar and also completely brand-new. I pulled out my phone and snapped a quick picture from my point of view of my empty couch adjacent. "Here!" I texted under the photo and pressed send to all: Mike, my siblings, my treatment team, and friends. I even sent it to both my parents' old cell phone numbers. Then I turned off the ringer and heard the waiting room door click open.

It was time.

And I was ready.

EPILOGUE

W e need to go back to the Cape."

My brother had called. It was time to clean out and sell the house.

"Okay, babe. We'll go," Mike said. "Are you sure it will be okay for you?" he asked, voicing the exact same concern my brother had.

Though I couldn't promise Mike, myself, or anyone else that I wouldn't get triggered or sick again, I felt the cells in my body being drawn to the Cape like a magnet.

We waited out the last days of school, packed up the car, and headed north. The minute I pulled our SUV into the sandy driveway of the beach house, the kids were tumbling out yelling in excitement. This time, they'd worn their suits in the car. Mike was right behind them. I sat motionless for a minute before finally cracking the driver's-side door, slipping off my shoes, and retracing last summer's footprints like a dog pacing out its territory. I walked to the same spot on the deck where I'd begun to fragment and splinter less than a year ago.

With the weather-beaten wooden boards finally back under my feet, the pain that had circled my heart for the better part of a year seemed to streak away like a gull toward the sea. I stretched my arms and legs and invited my body to expand into the space that knew me so well. I gulped my lungs full of the humid, salty air and noticed the presence of the new part of me I'd grown. The part that now carried and accepted my grief.

On the deck, I stood planted in the understanding that I had returned to strike the set of my childhood and the life my family had lived here together. Like a play I never imagined might end, this house, this beach, this town, was the stage that had hosted the comedies and tragedies of our lives. After more than thirty years it had finally fallen dark.

Being able to show up for this brutal task was a privilege I'd fought so hard for in treatment. I had different tools this time. I was different. I would take my leave of this little corner of earth with intention.

The house had belonged to another family before my parents bought it. The boards, pipes, and wires had outlived them all. Once it was cleared and cleaned out, and the paperwork was signed, the house would belong to a new family yet again.

I spent June and July going room to room, taking stock, sorting, tossing, and donating. Surrounded by the things that had once held so much meaning, I came to understand that we really don't own anything except our memories, and even those fade over time. Sometimes leaving a thing behind is actually just learning to live without it.

What I really wanted was the one thing I couldn't take—my mother's garden. It wasn't the flowers I cared about. I wanted the grass and the earth that had casually absorbed so many hours of her life.

The night before we left, I dreamed the steps where she'd walked and watered over three decades had been chalked across the lawn in footprints and arrows like an old-fashioned dance card. In my dream I threw myself on the ground, dug my hands into the earth, and ate the dirt. I shoveled the grass and sandy soil into my mouth by the fistful. I swallowed it dry.

When I woke at 3:00 a.m. I understood it was time to go. I knew I wouldn't fall back asleep. I'd gotten all I came for. There was nothing left but the phantom grit of the soil and seeds that clung to my teeth.

I waited for the blurry orange ball to break through the black horizon and announce the coming day. I dressed carefully, avoiding every creaky floorboard. I tiptoed through the home I had memorized, out the side door, across the dewy lawn, and down to the beach. The sun had risen. It was almost as though we had been waiting for each other.

At the ocean's edge I dipped my toes into the overly warm August water. Like an omen, I saw my very first jellyfish of the season—beautiful and venomous, floating in the inch of clear water just above the sandbar.

The sky unexpectedly darkened, and the sun found itself crowded out by rapidly gathering storm clouds. The wind picked up precipitously, and the waves capped in rolling curls of white. I felt a heavy raindrop and accepted it as my final cue.

Digging my heels into the wet sand, I spun around and walked back up to the deck of the beach house for the very last time.

I willed myself down into the wood and the sand and pulled into me the surrounding atoms from the sky above me and the earth beneath my feet. I blew my sudden tears into kisses and bowed as the ocean waves thundered me a standing ovation. I felt sure I could feel the energy that had once been my parents in the swirling wind. I grabbed fistfuls of air and gulped them in swallow after swallow until, as suddenly as it had begun, the wind died away. I gazed in reverence out at the mercurial sea.

"I will miss you for the rest of my life," I whispered.

The gray clouds separated slightly, and a bright stream of sunlight broke through. The light winked and dipped across the waves.

My mother's diamonds, of course.

On the very last day of the life that had once been mine, I walked myself off their deck and back up the hill toward Mike, our kids, and all the life we had ahead of us.

ACKNOWLEDGMENTS

Zibby Owens: You offered me hope when grief had me firmly by the hand. I am beholden to you. You have changed my life.

Zibby Books authors: Your extraordinary good company has been my great honor.

The Zibby Books team (past and present): You are an author's dream team come true. I am so grateful for your guidance (especially Kathleen Harris) and belief in this book.

Zibby's Book Club 2020: You were a light in a dark time. Thank you for giving me community when I needed it.

Pamela Cannon: Thank you for every kind word you ever said about my writing (they are tattooed on my heart). I loved you the most for every word you convinced me to cut.

Carolyn Murnick: You took an embarrassing tangle of chaos and taught me how to tell a story. I'm forever grateful.

Leigh Newman: Thank you for always telling me the truth. I love you as a writer, you terrify me as an editor, and you have my unwavering devotion forever.

ACKNOWLEDGMENTS

Joy Tutela: Thank you for believing in my writing and always telling it to me straight. You are a complete gift.

Jessica DuLong: My hometown hero and *Cinderella* castmate, thank you for your incredible book that I had to read out loud so I could be sure my mom got to hear it.

Lindsey Mead Russell: Thank you for the late-night Christmas text across continents and for being a lighthouse.

PEA women in pages: Thank you to our beloved Christine Shim, and to you all for bringing me back to the Harkness table full of brilliant women. Ale, thank you for always believing in me.

My Lamont crew—Lauren A., Leslie D., Megan D., Hania J., Anna K., Jamie F., Ale P.: You raised me. I owe a little bit of everything I've done since age fourteen to your love and care.

Matt Bays and Laura Parrot Perry: Thank you for loving me first and believing in me second. You are two of the most gifted writers I know.

Katherine Oelrich Welch: You gave me compass points, encouragement, and the Wailin' Jennys. I am forever indebted.

Diana Embry: I will always be grateful I said the f-word at that six-year-old's birthday party.

Christie Tate: It's not every day that a writer you stalked online becomes a real-life friend. Thank you for being real and generous and rooting for me. Thank you to the Friday writing group for accepting that I was a writer before I even did myself.

Glennon, Katherine, Liz, Gloria, Erin, Natalie, Abby, Sister, and the team at Together Rising: Thank you for giving me something to keep my hands busy when I felt the most helpless.

Stacy and Maribeth: Thank you for the support, friendship, and for keeping me afloat when I was sure I was sinking.

ACKNOWLEDGMENTS

Miles Adcox and your team at Onsite: You are a healing Oasis and I cannot imagine where I would be without you.

Chase S.: You threw me a lifeline when I needed it most.

Barri: Didn't the universe deal me such a good hand in you? Thank you for sitting next to me at Kripalu.

Julie R.: Thank you for being a third sister.

Nicole G.: Thank you for having the other crying baby in the mommy group.

Lisa P.—Birdo: I don't deserve you. I owe years of laughter to you. Thank you for letting me sleep on your futon.

Andrea A.: Truly, madly, deeply, thank you. You helped make D.C. my home.

Ladies Nighters: Thank you for the decades of support.

Susan B.: You are etched on the map of my life. Thank you for supporting me the way no one else ever could.

The Cotuit Contingent—the Burgesses, Churbucks, Fields, Berrys, Coppes, and Jacksons: Thank you for everything you have given and been to the entire Riordan family.

Baywatch Kate: The universe gave you to me like a present.

Gail: You, the porch, rosé, and cheese. That's all I need.

Crystal: You are the closest thing to love at first sight I've ever experienced. Your friendship has kept me afloat.

Nina Supana Flannery: Thank you for loving and raising these kids with me.

PQR: Thank you for offering a steady home base when the earth no longer tilted correctly on its axis.

BHR, AJR, SRN, CMR: I hope you will forgive me where it is required. Love you forever. And thank you for all of it.

The UK contingent—Hazel, Richard, Andrew, Yin, Chris, Anna, Tim, and Charlotte: Thanks for the love.

Julianne Rollefson: I am so proud of what we built. I can't remember how I did anything without checking with you first.

Rae: You told me I could do it before I even told you what I wanted to do. I love you.

Eva C.: You and our Sunday walks have been my church.

Laurie S: Thank you for always bringing the joy and the laughter, the stories and "boots do you stupid little pigs."

Sarah B.: When I look back across the most important moments of my life, I am so grateful to always see your face. Thank you for loving me through all my imperfections.

Pamela and Andy: Even being adjacent to your story has wrapped me in a lifetime of love. I hope I have been half the friend to both of you that you have always been to me.

MBF: This whole book is just a love letter to the universe that brought me you. I couldn't do any of it without you. I wouldn't even want to try.

MDJ: Thank you for showing me the true measure, the depth and breadth, of love. Thank you for never saying no and for backstopping all my shortcomings. You are my favorite.

Lucy, Daniel, and Nicky: I'm so grateful I get to hang with you. It's an honor to be your mom.

To the hundreds of clients who have invited me into their most intimate moments: It has been my greatest honor. I love you and am so proud to have known you.

And to my parents, Mary and John Riordan: I wish we had more time and that I had spent more of it thanking you.